Early Literacy
Materials Selector
ELMS

Early Literacy Materials Selector

ELMS

A Tool for Review of Early Literacy Program Materials

Kathleen Roskos

Lisa Lenhart

Brandi Noll

Foreword by Carol Vukelich

FOR INFORMATION:

Corwin

A SAGE Publications Company

2455 Teller Road

Thousand Oaks, California 91320

(800) 233-9936

www.corwin.com

SAGE Publications Ltd.

1 Oliver's Yard

55 City Road

London EC1Y 1SP

United Kingdom

SAGE Publications India Pvt. Ltd.

B 1/I 1 Mohan Cooperative Industrial Area

Mathura Road, New Delhi 110 044

India

SAGE Publications Asia-Pacific Pte. Ltd.

3 Church Street

#10-04 Samsung Hub

Singapore 049483

Acquisitions Editor: Jessica Allan

Associate Editor: Allison Scott

Editorial Assistant: Lisa Whitney

Production Editor: Amy Joy Schroller

Copy Editor: Terri Lee Paulsen

Typesetter: C&M Digitals (P) Ltd.

Proofreader: Caryne Brown

Indexer: Terri Corry

Cover Designer: Janet Kiesel

Permissions Editor: Karen Ehrmann

Printed in the United States of America

A catalog record of this book is available from the Library of Congress.

ISBN 978-1-4522-4164-7

This book is printed on acid-free paper.

12 13 14 15 16 10 9 8 7 6 5 4 3 2 1

Contents

Foreword

Every day a new catalogue appears in my mailbox, messages flash in my e-mail in-box, or my telephone voice mail light blinks telling of a message. The content is the same: A company spokesperson speaks convincingly of the merits of some new product. It *is* the right instructional material for your young learners. As the director of a project focused on early literacy working in several childcare centers, I'm targeted as someone with funds available to purchase, purchase, purchase. This is a luxury in early childhood education. Typically we have many needs for developmentally appropriate, educationally sound instructional materials and few dollars to meet our young learners' needs. In either condition, we must exercise care, great care, in what we select for use by and with our young learners.

Prior to these inventors' development of this tool, early childhood educators were faced with new instructional materials with no research-based tool to guide their review of the products. Now we have a tool to help us evaluate the quality of new (and well-worn) instructional materials along a variety of dimensions. The Early Literacy Materials Selector (ELMS) leads us through the challenging terrain of selecting the "just right" materials for our children. This manual begins by walking us through the variety of ways to use the tool, the range of materials that the tool could be used to review, and how to use the ELMS to enhance and extend professional learning. After building the *why*, it guides us through each component of our review of instructional materials. These inventors strongly believe that the instructional materials we use in our teaching matter.

Remember how Petunia thought she had knowledge when she carried a book under her wing and only later realized that she needed to actually *read* the words inside the book to be "in the know"? I'm feeling a bit like Petunia. ELMS has provided me with a means to open the cover and critically review each of the instructional materials I intend to purchase. How fortunate for me and for the young children with whom I have the privilege to work, play, and learn. Thanks to these inventors, I, like Petunia, am wiser!

—Carol Vukelich
Bruce L. and L. Sandra Hammonds Professor of Teacher Education
School of Education, University of Delaware

Preface

The Early Literacy Materials Selector presented in this book as Resource A is the result of numerous prototype drafts and revisions over five years of development. Its origins are in the sea change surrounding early literacy thought and policy at the start of the 21st century. A trilogy of research syntheses—*Preventing Reading Difficulties in Young Children* (Snow, Burns, & Griffin, 1998), *From Neurons to Neighborhoods: The Science of Early Childhood Development* (Shonkoff & Phillips, 2000, editors), and *Eager to Learn: Educating Our Preschooler* (Bowman, Donovan, & Burns, 2001)—shed new light on the significance of early literacy for school readiness and future reading achievement and sounded a clarion call for earlier, stronger, better literacy instruction. New preschool literacy programs and materials flowed into the school marketplace in response to the demand for more high-powered early literacy education. But few measuring sticks were available to gauge the quality of early literacy instructional materials for young children.

Early versions of the Early Literacy Materials Selector included criteria for reviewing curriculum elements (goals, objectives, learning activities, assessment) and guidance for instruction in essential early skills as defined by research. Referred to as the Early Literacy Program Review Tool (ELPRT), this prototype underwent several iterations over a three-year period based on desk and field studies, including testing of a CD-ROM version of this prototype (Roskos & Vukelich, 2007). Commentary from professional colleagues and feedback from helpful, thoughtful, patient educators led to the final ELMS prototype, which provides a good start for reviewing the range of early literacy instructional products and materials in early childhood classrooms. It is designed to offer a fairly short and efficient means of reviewing the quality features of instructional materials and making practical decisions about how to thoughtfully use them for purposes of preschool/early primary literacy instruction—a highly sensitive area of early childhood education given its foundational role in school literacy.

The *ELMS Early Literacy Program Materials Review Tool*—ELMS for short—has evolved over time thanks to the generosity of colleagues, educators, and teacher *friends* who have contributed their expertise, excellent thinking, and energy to its design. Their thoughtful observations have led to substantial revisions and improvements that make ELMS a viable tool. We look forward to new ideas, comments, and feedback from future colleagues who use ELMS in their professional work.

Several faithful professional friends have been involved from the start, and we extend a special thanks to them. Susan B. Neuman and Carol Vukelich contributed to the *idea* of a materials review tool and offered many insights on content and structure. Erin Wilson, a graduate student at the University of Delaware, spent nearly two years helping to transform the idea into *reality*: examining early literacy instructional materials, conducting literature reviews, helping to generate and categorize quality features, and applying features to numerous sample lessons. Mary Park, an instructional technologist in Edinburgh, Scotland, transformed the prototype from a paper-pencil version to a computerized version that made coding, tallying, and calculating more efficient and visually clear. Her work also illuminated the potentials and pitfalls of the ELPRT prototype.

While these professionals helped behind the scenes, others did so in the field—and we are grateful to them for their input. In particular, Christine Boivert, a preschool consultant for the early childhood team at the Oakland Schools in Waterford, Michigan, effectively tested the ELPRT prototype with teacher teams. Her efforts yielded a wealth of information about the technicalities of materials review, as well as possibilities for professional development in the systematic review of instructional materials. We wish to thank, as well, the preschool educators—Shelly Smith, Andi DeLap, and Erica Laughman—who applied ELMS to their early literacy instructional materials and reported their observations, concerns, insights, and "Aha!" moments in considerable detail. And our gratitude to our ever-patient literacy colleagues in the Akron Ready Steps program— Pat Bing, Shelley Houser, Pam Oviatt, Yu-Ling Yeh, Rozlyn Grant, and Linda Reesman—who tested various iterations of the tool time and again, and provided us with invaluable feedback every time.

There is the quote by Ralph Waldo Emerson: *Build a better mousetrap, and the world will beat a path to your door.* So it is . . . and after several years of trial and error, we have a much deeper appreciation of the *build* part in our attempt to design and develop a practical, usable product review tool for early educators who must make the best choices in early literacy instructional materials for young children.

Acknowledgments

Corwin gratefully acknowledges the contributions of the following reviewers:

Julie Frederick
Kindergarten Teacher
Seattle Public Schools
Seattle, Washington

Toni Jones
Superintendent
Falls Church City Public Schools
Falls Church, Virginia

Nicky Kemp
Elementary Principal
Williamsburg Elementary
Williamsburg, Missouri

Carol Olney
Early Intervention/Preschool
Teacher
Charleston County School District
Charleston, South Carolina

Sarah Switzer
Early Elementary Teacher
Farmer Elementary School,
Jefferson County Public Schools
Louisville, Kentucky

Heather Vaughn
Early Childhood Coordinator/
Curriculum Director
Albuquerque School District
Albuquerque, New Mexico

Sally Wingle
Preschool Teacher
Early Childhood Center
Chelsea School District
Chelsea, Michigan

About the Authors

Kathleen Roskos teaches courses in reading assessment and instruction at John Carroll University in Cleveland, Ohio. Formerly an elementary school reading teacher, Dr. Roskos has served in a variety of educational administration roles, including director of federal programs in the public schools, department chair in higher education, and director of the Ohio Literacy Initiative at the Ohio Department of Education. She has developed and coordinated numerous educational grants, most recently an online literacy specialist endorsement program. Dr. Roskos established one of the first public preschools in Ohio *(Bridges and Links)*. She has been instrumental in the design and development of statewide online professional development in reading for P–12 teachers. Her more recent activities involve professional development in Early Reading First programs in Arizona, New Mexico, and Ohio. Dr. Roskos studies early literacy development, teacher learning, and the instructional design of professional development for educators, and she has published numerous research articles, chapters, and books on these topics. She recently completed service as a lead writer of the 2010 Educator Professional Standards of the International Reading Association.

Lisa Lenhart is a professor in the College of Education at the University of Akron. She is currently the director of the college's Center for Literacy and is principal investigator on numerous grants. For the past several years she has been engaged in creating online professional development for teachers. She has coauthored several books, including *Oral Language and Early Literacy in Preschool* with Kathleen Roskos and *Reading and Learning to Read,* a popular textbook. Prior to her work at The University of Akron, Dr. Lenhart taught in Ohio's schools for more than 10 years. In her free time Lisa likes to read, bake, and hike. She is married to Matt and the mother of two daughters, Hannah and Emma.

 **Brandi Noll** is an assistant professor at Ashland University in Ashland, Ohio, where she teaches literacy courses. She is a former teacher, reading specialist, and literacy coach. Dr. Noll earned her Master's of Reading at Malone University in Canton, Ohio, and her PhD in Elementary Education with a focus on Literacy at The University of Akron in Akron, Ohio. Dr. Noll has presented both locally and nationally at a variety of literacy-related conferences, including the International Reading Association's National Conference. She has also published articles in a variety of journals and online sites. Dr. Noll lives near Canton, Ohio, with her husband and three children, and enjoys working on site with local teachers in order to bring research into their classrooms.

An Introduction to ELMS   1

Although teachers teach children, materials do matter.

We teach in an age of accountability. As educators seek ways to improve reading instruction for all children, they strive to implement evidence-based programs and techniques at all levels of instruction, recently referred to as tiers. (See, for example, www.rti4success.org/). In the search to implement the best practices for students who struggle (Tier 2, Tier 3), educators are rediscovering the power of everyday classroom instruction or Tier 1 as a strong antidote for reading failure. In districts, schools, and classrooms, educators are seeking answers to such questions as: What does Tier I instruction look like? What materials are used and in what way? Are the materials that teachers use guiding them *toward* or *away from* high-quality instructional practices? What many find in their search for answers is that:

1. The type and amount of materials currently being used by educators varies considerably from classroom to classroom and school to school.

2. Classroom instructional materials can range from teacher-made to professionally produced.

3. Publishing companies have labeled just about every product "research based."

4. With limited budgets, many schools want to ensure that they are getting their money's worth as they contemplate the purchase of new instructional materials.

Although there are probably few people who believe that materials *teach* students, many would agree that materials certainly *affect* teaching practices. Simply consider the following scenarios, and envision how instruction *might* be impacted by the quality and quantity of materials that a teacher uses:

- An urban Head Start preschool site provides each teacher with the newest comprehensive core program, which consists of a plethora of student books, big books, and high-quality literature;
- A suburban private preschool uses materials that teachers who started the school 30 years prior have created over the last couple of decades, simply passing these materials down like cherished family recipes;
- A small church-based preschool program has few resources except a handful of passed-down books, toys, and educational games;
- A rural preschool program purchased some commercially produced materials five years ago that were being promoted as "based on the latest research" and guaranteed to "promote optimum growth in all children"; however, most of the materials have been left to gather dust on the storage room shelves as teachers each pick and choose what they like the most.

Due to the lack of evidence about actual student outcomes within each of the scenarios above, we cannot judge how students might fare in each situation. Yet these examples serve to illustrate the fact that materials vary, and as a result it is likely that teaching and learning will vary. This realization about the variance in teaching material combined with the need to ensure that teachers are provided with materials and guidance that do indeed contribute to high-quality instruction has prompted the development of ELMS.

ELMS is a tool designed to assist early childhood educators and administrators in evaluating the quality and instructional guidance provided by early literacy curriculum materials and commercial programs. The ELMS tool offers a systematic approach to the review of early literacy curriculum materials based on evidence-based criteria of product quality. Its primary function is to check and critique the quality features of curriculum materials for product excellence as defined by the early literacy field. Developing an awareness of material quality is a good starting point as programs begin the process of critically analyzing tiered instruction within classrooms.

EARLY LITERACY MATERIALS: AREN'T THEY ALL THE SAME?

Materials are instructional resources that support instruction in an educational setting (Corcoran & Goetz, 1995). They are the durable goods of instruction, and include such items as teacher guides, student books, picture/word cards, posters, scope and sequence charts, among others tangible resources. Like all material things, instructional materials vary in quality, with some of higher caliber than others. In the pursuit of world-class early literacy instruction for all young children, the quality of curriculum materials matters. Access to high-quality curriculum materials affords teachers rich opportunities to develop supportive learning environments for young children and to plan and implement effective early literacy instruction. Moreover, in an era when strong Tier 1—or core—instruction in reading is the foundation of an effective early intervention system, the quality of materials takes on a new sense of urgency. The skilled carpenter knows that the quality of building tools and supplies makes a difference. So it is in early literacy teaching—the quality of curriculum materials matters, helping teachers deliver high-quality instruction.

The recent explosion in the number of commercially produced and prepackaged early literacy curriculum materials coincides with the growing recognition that learning to read and write begins early in life, and that preschool literacy experiences are influential in future literacy achievement (Dickinson & Neuman, 2006; Mol & Bus, 2011; Snow et al., 1998). Children's alphabet letter knowledge (letter names and sounds) at kindergarten entry, for example, is a significant predictor of success in the learn-to-read process in the primary grades (National Early Literacy Panel [NELP], 2009).

A variety of early literacy commercial programs and prepackaged curriculum materials offer preschool teachers ready-to-use sets of materials for helping young children learn early literacy skills. Still the convenience comes with a responsibility to make the best choices about the materials to be used with emerging readers and writers. Preschool educators need to consider how the materials function, as well as the guidance provided within the curricular materials, which directs teachers in how to use the materials most effectively.

WHO CAN USE ELMS AND WHY

Few tools are available today to assist early childhood educators in judging the quality of early literacy instructional materials. The ELMS tool

(Resource A) addresses this need. It is an easy-to-use tool that walks the reader through multiple evaluation steps and procedures designed to assist various stakeholders in completing a systematic review of core program materials and teacher guidance found within these materials.

ELMS is intended for those who design and implement early literacy programs, as well as those who are in decision-making roles about curriculum materials that are recommended for early literacy initiatives and projects, such as state education personnel, program proposal review panels, program administrators, project coordinators, and early literacy curriculum review teams. Teachers will also find the tool useful for reviewing their existing early literacy materials and in choosing new instructional resources for instruction.

WHAT DOES ELMS SERVE TO ACCOMPLISH?

ELMS is a practical tool. Its purpose, or function, is to check and critique the quality features of curriculum materials intended for use in early literacy instruction. We use the words *check* and *critique* deliberately here to indicate a process of (a) reviewing the internal qualities of a product and (b) observing its strong and weak features based on external criteria and standards grounded in a professional knowledge base.

To review the internal qualities of a program or set of curriculum materials, the ELMS tool checks the quality features of the materials contained in major categories of curricular resources, such as student materials. Users of ELMS are provided with all the tools and knowledge necessary to gather evidence of high-quality instruction in order to arrive at well-supported conclusions about the strengths and weaknesses of the early literacy materials under review.

WHAT DETERMINES HIGH QUALITY?

The goal of instructional design is to create high-quality, functional curriculum materials for purposes of instruction (Memmel, Ras, Jantke, & Yacci, 2007). The professional literature provides several sources of design criteria and standards for producing quality preschool literacy curriculum materials. Early childhood professional organizations (International Reading Association [IRA], 1998; NAEYC & NAECS/SDE, 2004), for example, regularly make recommendations related to appropriate early childhood literacy materials. The 1998 joint position statement of the International Reading Association and the National Association for the Education of Young Children set the criterion of sufficient instructional resources across several categories, including high-quality mixed-genre children's books, writing supplies, computer software, and multimedia resources at various levels of difficulty and reflecting various cultural and family backgrounds (IRA, 1998, p. 18).

Professional books also offer guidelines for the organization and content of preschool literacy materials. The National Research Council publication, *Starting Out Right: A Guide to Promoting Children's Reading Success* (Burns, Griffin, & Snow, 1999), for instance, listed general age-related recommendations about language and literacy materials and activities birth through Grade 3, including songs, rhymes and chants, games, play center materials, theme-based activities, books for shared reading, and multimedia. Other professional textbooks offer a combination of research-based findings and practical knowledge about creating, evaluating, and choosing curricular materials (e.g., Glover, 2009; McGee, 2007; Morrow, 2005; Neuman, Roskos, Wright, & Lenhart, 2007; Roskos, Tabors, & Lenhart, 2009; Schickedanz, 1999; Vukelich & Christie, 2009). See Resource B for a glossary of terms related to early literacy curriculum.

WHAT ESSENTIAL AREAS OF INSTRUCTION *SHOULD* INSTRUCTIONAL MATERIALS INCLUDE?

Theory and empirical research provide the foundations for identifying high-performing instructional practices found within early literacy curriculum materials. In the early literacy field, there is a growing consensus as to the body of knowledge and skills that form the basis of reading and writing ability (Dickinson & Neuman, 2006; Mol & Bus, 2011; National Reading Panel, 2000; NELP, 2009; Snow et al., 1998). To become a skilled reader, children need a rich oral language and conceptual knowledge base, a broad and deep vocabulary, and verbal reasoning abilities to understand messages that are conveyed through print.

Children also must develop code-related skills, an understanding that spoken words are composed of smaller elements of speech (phonological awareness); the idea that letters represent these sounds (the alphabetic principle), the many systematic correspondences between sounds and spellings, and a repertoire of highly familiar words that can be easily and automatically recognized (McCardle, Scarborough, & Catts, 2001). To attain a high level of skill, young children need opportunities to develop these strands, not in isolation, but interactively (IRA, 1998). Research syntheses describe early literacy content in several major skill categories that provide a foundational core for instruction (Bowman et al., 2001; Dickinson & Neuman, 2006; NELP, 2009; Rowe, 2008; Snow et al., 1998). These categories are briefly summarized in Figure 1.1.

Figure 1.1   The Content of Early Literacy

Alphabet Letter Knowledge

Alphabet letter knowledge includes letter name and sound knowledge, and the ability to retrieve this information quickly and accurately. Letter-name knowledge is one of the best predictors of future reading and spelling achievement not only in the primary grades, but also throughout elementary school, even into adulthood (Mol & Bus, 2011). It indicates early literacy exposure, helps children connect speech and print, and facilitates the acquisition of phonemic awareness. Children use their letter-name knowledge to learn letter sounds, and when fluent at letter naming they can pay more attention to decoding and storing words in memory, thus laying the foundation for single-word reading (Both-deVries & Bus, 2008). At the start of the learn-to-read process in preschool, children need rich exposure to alphabet letter names and sounds as tools for acquiring phonemic awareness and understanding the alphabetic principle (Neuman, Roskos, Wright, & Lenhart, 2007).

Phonological Awareness

Phonological awareness involves developing sensitivity to sounds in words and the ability to manipulate them. It demands a conscious attention to the sound structure of speech as opposed to its meaning, which is difficult for young children who are highly focused on meaning making in their environment. Research demonstrates the causal role of phonological awareness in reading acquisition since it permits children to understand the alphabetic principle—that sounds (phonemes) can be represented by letters (graphemes) (McBride-Chang, 1999). Rapid automatic naming—the ability to rapidly name a sequence of objects, letters, or digits—and phonological memory—the ability to remember spoken information for a short period of time—are also implicated in phonological awareness since these abilities can support or constrain focused attention to sounds in language (Torgensen, 2002; Wolf, Bally, & Morris, 1986). Phonological awareness is distinguished from phoneme awareness in that the former refers to a general awareness of the sound structure of oral language and the latter to the understanding that spoken words consist of individual sounds that can be analyzed and manipulated. At a prereading stage of reading development, the instructional focus is on phonological awareness, and in particular the abilities to distinguish sounds in the environment, recognize and produce rhyming words, segment words in sentences and syllables in words, and recognize repetitions of an initial consonant (Adams, Foorman, Lundberg & Beeler, 1998).

Print Knowledge

Print knowledge combines elements of alphabet letter knowledge, concepts about print, and early spelling. Broadly it includes conceptual knowledge of the purposes and conventions of print: concept of word; print awareness; and knowledge of reading terms, rules, and procedures. Print knowledge is moderately correlated with reading success, suggesting that it may be a proxy for print exposure and/or other early reading skill domains (e.g., alphabet letter knowledge) (Lonigan, Burgess, & Anthony, 2000). Given the scope of print knowledge in terms of specific abilities and skills related to learning to read, it is necessarily a large part of early literacy instruction embedded in shared reading and read-aloud activities that introduce and expose children to the nature and function of written language—stories, texts, sentences, and words (Justice & Vukelich, 2008).

Oral Language

Oral language constitutes a large domain of abilities significantly predictive of later reading achievement, including phonology, semantics, morphology, syntax, and pragmatics. As Perfetti (1987) argued, in the early phases of the learn-to-read process, "print is more similar to speech than speech is to print" (p. 356), thus abilities and skills of the more-familiar domain (oral language) are the most useful for problem solving in the less familiar domain (written language). In brief, children rely on their oral language knowledge to make sense of print, although their command of linguistic forms is tentative. Use of their oral language knowledge in print contexts is confronted by two challenges: the symbol-speech code and de-contextualized messages *in* print. Much preschool literacy instruction is focused on increasing the child's familiarity with print (the coding factor) and supporting meaning making with printed messages in stories, texts, and words (the contextual factor). Sharing quality books with children and developing listening comprehension skills are key instructional approaches that focus the child's attention on the code *and* the meaning embedded in print and picture.

Vocabulary

Vocabulary is a high priority in the early years because of its profound influence on both oral and reading comprehension over the life span (Hart & Risley, 1995; Marulis & Neuman, 2010). It refers to the words an individual knows and can use in speaking (expressive vocabulary) and/or recognized in listening (receptive vocabulary). The NELP (2009) synthesis of early literacy research argues that "building vocabulary alone" is likely insufficient for improving outcomes in early literacy skills, although it certainly is the "foundation for grammatical knowledge, definitional vocabulary and listening comprehension" (p. 75). Obviously if children have a poor vocabulary (store of words) they will encounter difficulties in both the oral and written conduits of communication. Research evidence shows that children's vocabulary store at age 3 predicts reading comprehension at Grade 3 (Biemiller, 2003; Hart & Risley, 2003). The preschool language and literacy curriculum, therefore, needs to be rich in vocabulary learning experiences that help children learn and understand many, many different kinds of words—basic concept words, root words, and disciplinary content words (Hirsch, 2006). Instruction should focus on helping children (1) acquire vocabulary through listening, speaking, shared reading, and writing; (2) develop their vocabulary consciousness—an awareness that words may have different meanings based on their context; and (3) cultivate a personal desire to learn new words (Biemiller & Boote, 2005; Silverman, 2007).

(Continued)

(Continued)

Writing

Early literacy researchers have developed an extensive research base describing 3- to 5-year-olds' hypotheses about writing, establishing that early writing behaviors mark the beginning of a learning trajectory that leads to more conventional writing and reading behaviors in the elementary school years (e.g., Clay, 1975; Ferreiro & Teberosky, 1982; Teale & Sulzby, 1986). Writing begins with scribbles that are largely undifferentiated and over time move in a general trajectory toward forms that have more writing-like characteristics, including linearity, appropriate directional patterns, and individual units (Levin & Bus, 2003). Preschoolers construct texts that reflect syntactic and semantic features of a variety of genres such as stories, lists, labels, signs, letters, and e-mails; they naturally combine writing, drawing, and other symbol systems, and their texts reflect flexible interweaving of semiotic systems (Rowe, 2008). The body of research on early writing establishes the importance of encouraging and assessing 3- to 5-year-olds' attempts at writing even before they begin to form conventional letters or spellings for words. Preschool writing instruction emphasizes language experience, shared writing, name-writing, and exploratory spelling attempts as the foundation of writing conventions and processes, as well as plenty of opportunities for children to compose texts that they dictate and/or write themselves as authors (Gentry, 2005; Glover, 2009; Rowe, 2008).

WHAT TEACHING PRACTICES *SHOULD* BE FOUND WITHIN INSTRUCTIONAL MATERIALS?

Instructional materials should promote strong pedagogy by incorporating effective teaching practices into the use of materials. Research supports systematic, sequential instruction in early literacy concepts and skills (Bowman et al., 2001; Frede, 1998; Pianta, Cox, & Snow, 2007), including all areas mentioned in Figure 1.2.

Figure 1.2 Early Literacy Teaching Practices

Environment

The systematic development of early literacy skills flourishes in a print-rich environment where there is an emphasis on oral-language development coupled with an emphasis on the foundational skills critical for grasping the alphabetic principle. Mixed-genre read-aloud books coordinated with content-rich units offer additional opportunities for developing children's vocabulary, phonology, syntax, and pragmatics that constitute strong language comprehension skills (Bowman et al., 2001; Snow et al., 1998). Opportunities for play, especially socio-dramatic play, provide meaningful contexts for practicing writing and reading skills, for exercising self-regulation abilities (Diamond, Barnett, Thomas, & Munro, 2007), and for using oral language in collaborative ways (Bodrova & Leong, 2007; Roskos & Christie, 2007). Intervention techniques that support children at risk and with special needs are also an integral part of effective early literacy instruction (Barnett, VanDerHeyden, & Witt, 2007).

Scope and Sequence

Additionally, the early literacy knowledge base supports a fairly well articulated scope and sequence for 4-year-olds in the development of phonological awareness, alphabet letter knowledge, vocabulary, print awareness, oral language abilities and skills, and writing (Burns et al., 1999; McBride-Chang, 1999; McGee, 2004; Treiman, 2000). While evidence is insufficient to determine an appropriate skill sequence for 3-year-olds, developmentally appropriate accomplishments have been identified, such as pretending to read, actively listening to stories, purposeful scribbling, and the like (Burns et al., 1999).

Lesson Framework

Effective teaching practice in early childhood pedagogy recommends a lesson framework that includes several key elements of instruction: (a) an explanation of the purpose of instruction, (b) direct teacher modeling, (c) interactive teacher-student practice, (d) instructional checkpoints, (e) application and practice of new information, and (f) periodic or cumulative review (Bohn, Roehrig, & Pressley, 2004; Strickland, 1989). To this purpose, early literacy instruction is generally organized around three instructional formats: Circle Time, Story Time, and Activity Time. An optimal amount of time for early literacy instruction has not been determined from research, but a 75- to 90-minute block of engaging language and literacy activities, including play time, appears productive (NELP, 2009).

Guidance

Teacher materials should provide planning guides for pacing daily instruction and notes for providing additional instruction as needed. Informal assessments should be used to make instructional adjustments in pacing, use of materials, and differentiating of instruction. In general, research shows the value of well-paced instruction that is supported by ongoing progress monitoring for making adjustments suited to student needs (Foorman & Torgeson, 2001; Wiggins & McTighe, 2007).

Differentiated Instruction

Differentiated instruction is a teaching theory based on the premise that instructional approaches should vary and be adapted in relation to individual and diverse students in classrooms (Tomlinson, 2001). The purpose of differentiating instruction is to maximize each student's growth and individual success by meeting each student where he or she is and assisting in the learning

(Continued)

(Continued)

process; it means tailoring instruction to meet individual needs. Differentiated instruction is grounded in the work of Vygotsky's (1978) zone of proximal development (ZPD), which is the range at which learning takes place. Some of the first classroom research to support the concept of ZPD was done by Fisher et al. (1980) (cited in Hall, Strangman, & Meyer, 2011). Other practices have been noted as central to differentiation and have been validated in the effective teaching research (Ellis & Worthington, 1994). Based on this knowledge, the goal of differentiated instruction is to give students multiple options for taking in information and making sense of ideas. The model of differentiated instruction requires teachers to be flexible in their approach to teaching, and adjust the curriculum and presentation of information to learners rather than expecting students to modify themselves for the curriculum. For the preschool curriculum, this means that materials need to be inclusive to enough to meet the needs of all students yet flexible enough for teachers to make informed decisions for individuals. Additionally, the curriculum needs to offer a variety of media, such as books, manipulatives, and online resources to meet students' various learning styles.

HOW IS THE ELMS TOOL ORGANIZED?

The design of the ELMS tool is grounded in the knowledge bases of early literacy learning and teaching. The tool includes an inventory for itemizing the materials contained in a program, eight categories of curriculum materials that reflect the material contents of a program, and seven domains of evidence-based practice that identify the early literacy skill instructional content of a program. The basic design of the tool is outlined in Figure 1.3.

ELMS is organized into four parts. Part I consists of an *Inventory of Materials* that identifies primary items and how many are available for instruction, as well as the type of program under review. Items are organized into eight categories of primary items commonly found in sets of curriculum materials and programs. These categories include Teacher Materials, Student Materials, Curriculum Descriptions, Scope and Sequence, Assessment Materials, Home-School Materials, Multimedia, and Professional Development Materials. Completing this section of the tool is an important first step in unpacking a set of curriculum materials and helps reviewers to become familiar with the material contents of a program. Commercial and prepackaged programs vary considerably in the types and amounts of materials that are provided for early literacy instruction.

Part II provides criteria for rating the *quality of materials* contained in a program or curriculum set within the eight categories. The reviewer

Figure 1.3 Design of the ELMS Tool

I. Inventory of Materials

Materials Present and Amount

- Teacher Materials
- Student Materials
- Curriculum Descriptions
- Scope and Sequence
- Assessment Materials
- Home-School Materials
- Multimedia
- Professional Development Materials

Type of Program

II. Categories of Curriculum Materials

Availability, Capacity, and Usability

- Teacher Materials
- Student Materials
- Curriculum Descriptions
- Scope and Sequence
- Assessment Materials
- Home-School Materials
- Multimedia
- Professional Development Materials

III. Evidence-Based Practice Domains

Presence of Evidence-Based Practices

- Oral Language
- Vocabulary
- Phonological Awareness
- Alphabet Letter Knowledge
- Print Knowledge
- Writing
- Differentiated Instruction

IV. Quality Performance Rating

- Exceptional
- Very Good
- Good
- Low

rates the primary material items in each category on three criteria: (1) availability of items, that is, what items a category contains; (2) capacity, that is, that the primary items are available in a sufficient amount to accomplish effective instruction; and (3) usability, which describes the practical characteristics of the primary items available in terms of construction, appropriateness, and appeal. Each criterion uses a 0–3 scale to qualitatively rate the primary items in a category.

Part III, referred to as *Analysis of Guidance,* provides a method for systematically examining the set of directions or guidance provided to inform instruction in seven early literacy skill domains that are the focus of evidence-based practice, including Oral Language Comprehension, Vocabulary, Phonological Awareness, Alphabet Letter Knowledge, Print Knowledge, Writing, and Differentiated Instruction. To conduct an analysis of guidance, the reviewer chooses a sample of lessons or activities from the set of materials/program. Most often, lessons or activities are described in the teacher guide or manual. For each lesson or activity, the reviewer searches for and locates the presence of key instructional items (best practices) in the seven early literacy skill domains. A total of 20 items are identified across seven evidence-based early literacy domains. The reviewer determines if the items are present in a sample lesson and computes the average for each skill domain in a set of sample lessons.

Part IV of the tool provides an overall rating of product quality, referred to as *Quality Performance Rating.* In this final application of the tool, the reviewer computes the average of percentages scores from Parts II and III. The total percentage score total is then placed on a continuum to indicate "exceptional," "very good," "good," or "low" overall product quality performance. The reviewer can immediately see the potential of a set of materials/program as a resource that supports teachers in achieving the goal of excellent preschool literacy instruction for young children.

CHAPTER 1 REVIEW

More than ever, educators need tools to help them examine and review the material resources they use for instruction. Quality materials in capable hands can make a difference in creating a nurturing and enriching literacy learning environment. The ELMS tool is designed to inventory the materials in a program in eight commonly used categories and to rate their quality in terms of availability, capacity, and usability. It provides a framework for reviewing the quality of the instructional guidance according to evidence-based domains of early literacy skill and practice. Based on these analyses, the reviewer can assess the overall quality performance of a product and its potential for use in a local setting. The first step is considering who will take part in the review and then determining what will be reviewed. Chapter 2 will help guide you in making these important decisions.

Planning a Review   2

Sometimes the hardest part is just getting started!

Getting started with a review is an important first step—like the journey of a thousand miles that starts with a *single step*. When you purchased this tool, you may have already had a plan in place for how you were going to conduct your review. On the other hand, you may have simply arrived at the decision that you had materials that needed review, but you weren't quite sure how to accomplish this feat. The purpose of this chapter is to provide the reader(s) with a variety of options and suggestions for using ELMS to review curricular materials. There really is no one right way to use the tool, as it provides much flexibility so that it can be used in a variety of situations and for a variety of purposes.

In the first section of this chapter, suggestions are provided for who might be involved in a review. In the second section of the chapter, the types of programs that could be reviewed are explained.

WHO WILL PARTICIPATE IN THE REVIEW?

There are three basic approaches to a product review using the ELMS tool: a "team" approach, "small group" approach, or "on your own" approach. Each has its benefits and drawbacks. A team approach fosters collaboration and joint professional learning, although assembling a diverse team of stakeholders and finding time to work together may be challenging. A small-group approach is less formal, easier to manage, and also fosters collaboration, but it can be limited in terms of input and time to do the job well. Approaching this on your own has the benefit of independence and flexibility, but it can lack perspective—not to mention the burden of sole responsibility for getting the job done. The ELMS tool can be effectively applied in each approach—but the decision for *how to* conduct a review using the tool rests with local educators and is dependent on time, resources, and educational purposes. A few ideas for each approach are described in the sections below. Additionally, a set of checklists and organizers is located in Resource E.

A Team Approach

Assembling a group of educators into a high-functioning team tasked with a curriculum product review can be challenging. Consider who will lead the team and the group members, establish the goals and priorities of the review, and create a timeline. Be mindful that a quality review depends on a quality team; thus members need to be clear as to their charge, knowledge, collaborative ability, and commitment to the task; a strong, well-organized team chair is critical. The team should be fully aware of the curriculum policies of the agency and/or school as they enter into a review. Educational needs of children need to be identified, as well as the specific instructional goals of the educational program. In Resource F you will find a descriptive case study of one such team review.

Small-Group Approach

Small informal work groups, consisting of two to three members, are easily formed in most settings. The keys here are to ensure that the participants are willing to take on the responsibility of a review and commit to the time it will require, and that the leadership will use the outcomes of the review in curriculum decision making and future product purchasing. The leadership should set a time frame for the review and lay out expectations about reporting by the group to supervisors and peers.

On Your Own Approach

In some situations, neither the team nor the small-group approach is feasible for conducting a review, and the responsibility rests solely on an individual. Individual teachers can use the ELMS tool to review the program materials used in their particular classroom. This provides an opportunity to inventory the material contents of a program at hand; to survey what is available and judge whether there is enough to do the job and how usable items are; and to analyze the guidance for its accuracy, completeness, and trustworthiness with respect to instructional direction.

In other instances, an administrator or supervisor may want to review a new literacy program or combination of materials being considered for purchase in the local site. In these *on your own* situations, the outcomes of the review can inform daily instructional decision making, as well as curriculum planning by leadership.

Any of these previously mentioned approaches might include such stakeholders as preschool teachers, literacy specialists or coaches, administrators, curriculum specialists, and board members.

WHAT TYPES OF PROGRAMS CAN BE REVIEWED USING ELMS?

The basic premise of the ELMS tool is that materials matter in the delivery of early literacy instruction. Good teachers make good use of good materials. An ELMS review can aid early childhood educators in determining the strengths, weaknesses, and overall qualities of early literacy materials in the programs described in Figure 2.1.

In the following section, the application of the ELMS tool is discussed in conjunction with the four major program types (published, embedded, prepackaged assortment, and mixed assortment), illustrating how the tool helps educators review materials relevant to their local situation.

Figure 2.1 Types of Program Materials

- **Publisher-based early literacy program** that provides a curriculum framework for early literacy teaching and learning; it contains a coordinated set of commercially produced materials available *off the shelf* as a total package. A popular example is *Opening the World to Literacy* (OWL; 2005) published by Pearson.
- **Embedded early literacy program** that is inserted into a comprehensive early childhood curriculum, such as *Creative Curriculum* (Dodge, Colker, Heroman, & Bickart, 2002). It contains a coordinated set of commercially prepared materials available *off the shelf,* but the set is adapted and modified to *fit* with the broader curriculum; some material resources are used (e.g., big books), but not others (e.g., software).
- **Prepackaged assortment of materials** that is used to assemble an early literacy program; it contains a variety of commercially produced materials available *off the shelf* that provide a collection of learning activities in early literacy skills.
- **Mixed assortment of prepackaged and teacher-made materials** that is used to assemble an early literacy program; it contains a mix of commercially produced materials available *off the shelf* as singular items and teacher-made materials that constitute the instructional delivery in early literacy.

Publisher-Based Programs

Publishers currently market prepackaged, comprehensive language and literacy programs for the early childhood setting. Most programs claim to be research based yet differ in the amount of materials available, instructional practices, and supportive materials for purposes of assessment and instruction. Programs also vary in cost, with some considerably more expensive than others. Purchasing a new program for an entire staff is a major commitment, and every effort should be made to ensure that the instructional materials are appropriate for those it is intended to serve. Teams consisting of administrators, early literacy specialists, curriculum directors, and teachers can work together to review different programs using the ELMS tool. We caution against making decisions based on a single score. Rather by recording notes, questioning, analyzing findings, and taking into account prior experience, educators can use their best judgment to select instructional materials that are the best fit for a local setting.

The following example illustrates the use of ELMS in selecting new materials. A large, county preschool system is preparing for the future purchase of new literacy materials for its twenty-six sites using funds provided through a state-supported literacy initiative grant. Current materials are more than seven years old, and the entire staff agreed that these materials did not reflect best practices in preschool literacy. Since the initiative involved spending a large sum, administrators agreed that just any off-the-shelf program would not do. A committee, consisting of teachers, literacy experts, and administrators, was formed to study commercial programs on the market. After eliminating a few programs poorly suited to the schools' needs, three commercial programs were considered for a more in-depth analysis using the ELMS tool. Three-member teams applied the tool to evaluate the commercial programs. Each team evaluated program materials and presented observations to the other teams. Two programs demonstrated comparable scores and by far outperformed the third. Teams went back through their notes of the high-performing programs and found that despite comparable scores, the programs varied in strengths and weaknesses. In the end, the teams agreed to purchase one of the high-performing programs, well aware of its drawbacks. The teams decided that the next step was to identify practical ways to augment the program.

Embedded Literacy Programs

The ELMS tool can be used to review early literacy programs that are integrated into a comprehensive curriculum framework. Many preschool settings struggle with funding issues that limit purchasing new, complete early literacy commercial programs. Some simply have to *make do* with partial sets of program materials. ELMS can be used to examine current literacy materials for alignment with research in early literacy teaching. School personnel can then determine whether the overall comprehensive program needs to be adjusted and in what ways. A program evaluation using the ELMS tool may help the staff discover what areas need to be supplemented or completely replaced.

Consider this example. Training at a local Head Start consisted of the most recent research on essential early literacy skills published in the report of the National Early Literacy Panel (NELP, 2009). Teachers were using an outdated set of published literacy materials interwoven with a comprehensive curriculum. In discussing the panel report, the teachers realized that their program was seriously lacking in several areas of reading readiness, including alphabet knowledge, concepts of print, vocabulary, memory, and phonological awareness. They decided that they needed to carefully select supplemental materials to bolster their in-place instructional resources in order to deliver a stronger early literacy program. They also observed that reliable, valid early literacy progress monitoring was needed to differentiate instruction and to guide materials selection for this purpose. In this case, the review tool helped the teachers to observe the strengths and weaknesses of their instructional materials and to make decisions about the future purchase of curricular resources.

Prepackaged Assortment of Materials

Sometimes educators face a blessing of riches where instructional materials are abundant, having built up over the years or having increased due to grant awards and one-time initiatives. To use all would require more instructional time than is available, overwhelm other curricular areas, and perhaps lead to unnecessary duplication. The ELMS tool can be used to evaluate assorted sets of curriculum materials toward the goal of streamlining a collection into a coherent set of resources. The *inventory*, for example, can be used to itemize materials, identify duplicates, and indicate primary areas of emphasis. It can be the first step in sifting out materials for further review and those that can be eliminated from consideration. The *quality of materials rating* and *guidance analysis* can further "weed out" supportive from nonsupportive materials that do not contribute to instructional goals.

Consider this scenario. At a local, private preschool, classrooms and the resource room were overflowing with instructional materials. As a result, teachers used a wide variety of materials, usually those they had grown familiar and comfortable with over the years. A teacher in a master's degree program noticed that some essential literacy skill instruction she was learning about were not evident in the most-used instructional materials. She also began to notice that two programs she was using in combination duplicated instruction across the preschool day. After she brought her observations to the attention of her administrator, the pair concluded that there was a definite need to formally sort through the wide array of materials being used in classrooms. The entire staff used the ELMS tool to evaluate the instructional materials they were using in their own classrooms. What teachers found startled them! Some teachers were devoting much of their time instructing on a few skills, such as oral language comprehension, print knowledge, and phonemic awareness, while others spent considerably less time on other essential skill areas, such as alphabet knowledge. It was also discovered that materials used for developmental writing were outdated and not representative of current research. ELMS helped these teachers *to step back* from their daily teaching to evaluate their instructional choices and how these shaped what they were doing for much of the day.

Mixed Assortment Programs

Many preschool programs use a combination of instructional materials gathered from prepackaged commercial materials and/or teacher-made sources. There are real reasons for this patchwork approach to early literacy materials for instruction, not the least of which is the underfunding of early childhood programs. Yet it is risky because high-quality early literacy instruction depends, in part, on high-quality materials designed and developed by highly knowledgeable early literacy professionals. This is a primary reason for a tool like ELMS, which can help preschool directors and teachers evaluate a mixed set of instructional materials. First, it can help staff inventory what they have and what they don't have in terms of instructional resources. Second, it can survey those materials that are regularly used. And third, it can help staff analyze the quality of program guidance made available to teachers who rely on the materials in the delivery of instruction. The tool can make visible areas of strength and gaps in early literacy instruction.

This example is illustrative. A small, nonprofit preschool hired a new administrator who was unfamiliar with the instructional materials used for preschool literacy instruction. Over time she noticed that a variety of commercial products and teacher-created materials were being used intermittently. She worried that the conglomeration of instructional materials may not be addressing essential literacy skills. Teams of teachers and teachers' aides evaluated the mixed set of materials to judge comprehensiveness. Five teams, each made up of two teachers and/or aides, applied the ELMS tool to different sets of materials. After each team had completed its review, teams met to compare their results. The evidence was clear: material resources neglected differentiated instruction and developmental writing. Action steps were developed to plan for professional development and to identify materials to address neglected areas.

CHAPTER 2 REVIEW

Different approaches can be used to apply the ELMS tool, from formalized teams or committees to informal small work groups to individual review. Each approach has its merits and offers opportunities not only to examine material resources but also to grow professionally. Across these different approaches, the tool supports the review of different program types that are commonly found in early childhood settings. Examples of reviews in four major early literacy curricular materials types illustrate the different uses of the tool toward a common goal of product review. In the next chapter, we explore how ELMS can also be used for professional development, teacher preparation, and curriculum development.

More Than a Simple Review of Materials

3

The process of evaluating materials often provides an opportunity to learn more than the end product alone can teach us.

In the previous chapters, we have described the *what* and *how* of the ELMS tool as a means for reviewing the quantities and qualities of a set of curriculum materials. The tool, however, has utility beyond the scope and purpose of a review. The tool not only helps educators learn about the potentials of materials for instruction but also helps them learn from the experience of examining and reviewing materials as the durable goods of instruction. In this section we explore three additional uses of the ELMS tool that enhance and extend professional learning: in professional development, in teacher preparation, and in curriculum development.

PROFESSIONAL DEVELOPMENT

The ELMS tool can be used in conjunction with, or as a springboard for, professional development in essential areas of preschool literacy education. For teachers and professionals, the process of using the tool to evaluate a set of materials can be a valuable professional learning experience in and of itself. Often, when new instructional materials are adopted, teachers receive only minimal training on how to use the materials. Most often, sales personnel facilitate half-day training that involves a mere "unpacking" and surface exploration of the inner workings of the program. Teachers are often provided little time to explore the program's guidance in essential components in-depth before using it in their classrooms. Guiding teachers in the use of the ELMS tool and including them in all steps of the evaluation process affords them a critical look at the design, components, and practices embedded within the set of materials. They afford opportunities for them to explore, question, analyze, and reflect on the quantities and qualities of the instructional materials.

While using the ELMS tool, professional development needs can be uncovered. During the review, discussions between staff members can enlighten leaders about any literacy areas that are weak among staff. For example, when using the vocabulary section within Part III, teachers may ask questions inquiring about the term "vocabulary consciousness" and the phrase "clear procedures for vocabulary instruction." In response to these conversations, professional development can be planned and tailor-made to address specific needs of the staff and at the same time deepen teacher knowledge about an essential early literacy skill domain.

Consider another example, which illustrates how the ELMS tool supports in-progress professional development in early literacy and can also stimulate new professional development initiatives. At a large Head Start center, teachers are involved in using ELMS to evaluate their current early literacy program—facilitated by the program director and the early literacy coach. Before using the ELMS tool, teachers reviewed its content, discussed what the term *best practices* meant, and shared how to identify evidence of *best practices* in program guidance documents. Guiding these discussions, the director and coach remained alert to key topics of conversation, confusions, and puzzlements. Following the application of the tool and debriefs on the results, the coach strategically started new conversations with the staff around confusing areas of practice and how to use materials more productively. Professional development was then planned that addressed the teachers' weakest areas in relation to the knowledge areas and instructional approaches. Review and use of the tool was both situated within and a springboard for new professional learning experiences.

Whether ELMS is used to assess a current or future commercial program, a collection of several purchased programs, or teacher-created materials, it is critical that those staff members who are or will be using the materials be part of the review process. By becoming involved with the process, teachers are afforded the opportunity to sort out what instructional practices are integral to any early literacy program and what these instructional materials are designed to provide. Left out of this process, teachers have little opportunity to observe overlooked, yet essential, areas of instruction; literacy or instructional areas receiving more attention than others; and possibly the overall balance of skill-based instruction versus meaning-related instructional practices. Teacher involvement from the get-go supports the immediate identification of practical teaching problems that lead to targeted professional development. A knowledgeable practitioner in each setting should be identified to ensure informed decision making in choosing materials.

TEACHER PREPARATION

The ELMS tool can also be used in the preparation of preservice teachers and during graduate-level workshops or coursework. Upon entering the field of education, teachers are often simply presented with a set of curriculum materials with the expectation that these materials be implemented immediately and occasionally with strict fidelity. Sometimes these materials are purchased curriculums, or hand-me-downs from colleagues, and in other instances, teachers must go out on their own to gather and purchase necessary curriculum and resources. No matter how curriculum materials end up in their hands, it is vital that teachers have the knowledge and tools necessary to evaluate the quality and comprehensiveness of these materials. Teachers should not be expected to simply "follow the script" of curriculum materials without being critical of the quality of the features of the program.

So, in preparation for making these vital decisions upon entering the field of education, preservice teachers who are learning about early literacy can use the tool in coordination with their coursework to investigate instructional practices within preschool curriculum. For example, a person studying to become a preschool teacher can use the tool to evaluate, compare/contrast, and assess guidance within commonly used materials in area preschools. The instructor of the course serves as the facilitator or coordinator of such an exercise, guiding the preservice teacher through the evidence or guidance that a program features, while supplementing with additional texts and scholarly articles to help build the knowledge base in various early literacy constructs. Information gained while exploring the curricular materials can be used as a springboard for class discussions and assignments.

The tool can be used in-depth while also studying some or all essential early learning areas included in the tool. For example, a group of preservice students might work together to compare the writing instruction found in a variety of programs during a course designed to focus on developmental writing in the preschool years. Using what they are learning in this course, preservice teachers can evaluate the instructional guidance in writing contained in early literacy curriculum materials. Teams of students then pull examples of teacher guidance from the teacher manuals and critique them, while considering what they are learning about effective practices within the teacher preparation course. By participating in these evaluative critiques, preservice teachers are better prepared to make sound decisions in regard to curriculum materials once they enter the workforce.

In a similar way, practicing teachers who use the ELMS tool in their graduate-level coursework can become more cognizant of the curricular materials they use in their own classrooms. Often, teachers become so overburdened with management tasks such as paperwork and other noncurricular busywork that they are left with little time to explore and evaluate the quality of the program materials presented to them for classroom use. Curricular materials can also be simply provided to the teachers for classroom use, while the need for professional development designed to help them choose instruction guidance and materials wisely from the curriculum available for use may be neglected. Unfortunately, although many curriculums have been designed using a common bank of research in the field of early learning, instructional strategies and materials can vary widely. No program is perfect, and each one varies in its quality of materials and guidance, as well as strengths and weaknesses. Therefore, these materials should be carefully evaluated and explored by stakeholders such as teachers, parents, principals, and governing bodies in the preschool setting.

Below you will find a few suggestions for activities that can be used in either teacher-preparatory or graduate-level courses.

Activity 1: Preservice Teachers

As preservice teachers spend time in the field, ask them to record observational notes in regard to instructional materials used by the off-site teachers and students. Each time preservice teachers visit the cooperating school, direct them to complete one section of the ELMS tool. For example, they could use the inventory to explore what materials are provided, or one section of the quality analysis, and so on. Upon completion of each section, students can share their discoveries and reactions during class discussion. Discussions can focus on the quality of program materials and guidance in various early literacy areas in relation to the content covered within the course.

Activity 2: Practicing Teachers

Explore the ELMS tool in a graduate-level course. Have practicing teachers choose and use one section of the tool each week to evaluate the usefulness and effectiveness of the curriculum materials they currently use. After completing each section, class discussion can provide a time for teachers to reflect on and discuss their use of the curricular materials as well as their findings in regard to their quality.

Activity 3: Preservice or Practicing Teachers

As preservice or practicing teachers complete the ELMS tool, have them explore and discuss weak areas found within the curricular materials they evaluated. In light of their findings, ask them to search for curricular materials that can be used to supplement the program in the areas of deficit, or to design supplemental, research-based lessons that can be integrated with the curricular materials that were evaluated.

Activity 4: Preservice or Practicing Teachers

Before having preservice or practicing teachers use the ELMS tool, have them contact a local sales representative who works for a specific preschool curriculum publishing company. Ask them to interview the sales representative to find out what the company claims are the benefits of using their program. Ask the representative for samples of the program materials that can be explored by the students in the course. Using the sample curriculum materials, have students work in teams to use the ELMS tool to evaluate all components of the program materials. Thereafter, have students evaluate whether the sales representative's claims about the program match what the students have found using ELMS. This exercise can lead to an enlightening conversation about the claims that publishers can make in regard to the published programs.

Activity 5: Preservice or Practicing Teachers

Students in undergraduate or graduate-level literacy courses can conduct a personal interview with an administrator at a local preschool. For this interview, the student should develop and ask specific questions that inquire about the process that the organization takes to adopt curricular materials. Questions should investigate the process that local organizations take to ensure that the materials that teachers use are of the highest quality. Specific questions can be developed using the ELMS tool as a model. For example, using the section designed to set a purpose and goal for the use of the tool, students in the course might ask the program coordinator what goals they have when adopting new materials.

CURRICULUM DEVELOPMENT

Faced with the challenge of better early literacy education for all young children, there is a growing need for language-rich, rigorous, and engaging reading curricula that prepare them for school. But it is unrealistic to expect early childhood teachers to both design *and* deliver high-quality curricula every day. The practicality of the matter is that teachers need ready access to early literacy materials they can trust and easily use. But to achieve this goal, educators and teachers need guidance that helps them to ground curriculum selection on evidence. A review of a curricular resource using the ELMS tool provides the kind of reliable information early educators and teachers need to make well-informed decisions about materials and products for early literacy instruction.

Here is a case example. In an Early Reading First program referred to as Akron Ready Steps, the leadership, literacy coaches, and teaching staff created an integrated early literacy curriculum that is content based. They organized early literacy teaching and learning into two integrative parts in which children can experience direct instruction in both rich content and essential skills. This approach affords simultaneous access to disciplinary content and early literacy cognitive processes, thus increasing the efficiency and potential effectiveness of curriculum. In practical terms, teaching and learning activities are organized around a topic study (e.g., buildings), and primary curricular materials are aligned to this inquiry, including literacy resources. The ELMS tool is used to inform this curricular work, serving as a framework to guide the selection of material items for instructional delivery and to monitor the quality and emphases of instructional direction in daily practice. In this application, the tool provides the necessary feedback for ongoing program monitoring.

CHAPTER 3 REVIEW

In a fast-paced world, tools that can multifunction and multitask are preferred. The aforementioned scenarios illustrate how the ELMS tool has the potential to lead, teach and serve. It can be used as a tool in the evaluation of early literacy curriculum; it can be used to chart a professional development curriculum; it can be used as a teaching resource in professional education; it can serve as a framework in guiding and monitoring curriculum design. In all these ways, the tool shows its potential for making a real contribution to strong early literacy education. In the next chapter you will learn about Part I of the ELMS tool.

Taking Inventory of Teaching Materials   4

Taking inventory is much like excavating prehistoric dinosaur fossils—each discovered piece contributes toward the creation of the dynamic whole.

An ELMS review begins with Part I, an inventory that describes what material items are available for a review. An inventory allows the reviewers to take stock of the actual contents of an early literacy program or set of curriculum materials. It organizes and lists materials by type and amount, that is, *what* items and *how many* constitute the program contents.

The ELMS inventory is organized into eight categories of materials commonly found in early literacy programs (see Figure 4.1). To ensure a thorough and systematic review, all material items should be gathered together before conducting a review. If all materials are not present, note that the set is incomplete. Even if the review will not be conducted in one sitting, it is best to assemble the materials together in one place. A sound review depends on easy access to a complete set of materials.

Before starting an inventory of items, provide identifying information about the program or set of materials on the cover page of the tool (see Figure 4.2). Record the name of the product and the publisher. If the program and/or set include multiple products, list the publisher of each product. Locate the date(s) of publication for each product. The copyright

Figure 4.1 Categories of Materials for Review

Category	Description
Teacher Materials	Resources used by the teacher that guide and aid instruction, such as teacher guides, sets of word cards, big books, read-aloud books, charts, and the like
Student Materials	Resources intended for student use with or without the teacher, such as little books, manipulatives (e.g., letter tiles), and student-reproducible books or practice pages
Curriculum Description	Explanation of the research base, program goals, links to standards, and descriptions of major instructional activities
Scope/Sequence	Describes what should be taught and when, in a chart or table
Assessment Materials	Assessment tasks with directions, student forms, record forms, and interpretations of results; these may be used for progress monitoring
Home-School Materials	Resources that support the curriculum at home, such as parent letters, activities/games for home, and tips for parents
Multimedia	Resources that provide multimodal learning experiences via software, CDs/audiotapes, DVDs, and e-books
Professional Development Materials	Resources that support teacher learning, such as research summaries, models of instructional sequences, and recommendations for professional resources

date can be tricky to find and may not be located on the copyright page. Search through the front and back matter of the program guide to locate a publication date. If finding this date is difficult, a phone call to the publishing company, a visit to the website, or even a product catalogue can usually offer some clues as to publication date. Additionally, on the front cover page there is an area designed for recording the name of the reviewer and the date on which the reviewed occurred.

Figure 4.2 Example of Identifying Information

Product Name	Publisher	Copyright Date
XYZ Program	L&R School Products	2004
Alphabet Fun	L&R School Products	2005
Storybook Kit	Noll Associates	2007

Locating the copyright date is important! A popular preK series, for example, was published in 2005, but updated in 2007 with new supplementary materials. When the 2007 edition was ordered by a preschool program for review, there was confusion until a quick call to the publisher clarified that the core materials were the same but the new edition provided additional supplementary materials. Also determine if the review is focusing on outdated materials that may not adequately represent current early literacy research. On the flip side, new editions may tout *bells and whistles,* links to early learning standards, and connections to the research base, yet close inspection may reveal gaps.

COMPLETING THE INVENTORY

Completing the ELMS inventory is easy and straightforward. It requires that the reviewer identify the types and amounts of materials available for review in each category. Counting the number of items is not relevant or appropriate within some categories; therefore, the term *not applicable* (recorded as *NA*) appears in the *Amount* column. A sample inventory for a fictitious program is illustrated in Figure 4.3. Keep in mind that the inventory is not intended to rate the *quality* of the materials available; that task is addressed in Part II of the tool. The inventory is simply designed to determine the material items available for a review.

If those conducting the review have already been using the program, completing the inventory will move quickly. In this case, the only surprise may come if reviewers notice that there are material items in the program that have not been used. Items previously purchased may have been overlooked or ignored by staff. In cases where material items contained in a new program are under consideration for purchase, the inventory may take longer to complete. The time spent inventorying the program materials, however, is time well spent—even though a bit daunting when reviewers face the many pieces and parts of some programs.

The best approach to completing the inventory is to work through each category and the related material items one at a time. Check if items are available in a category, and then record how many are available for review. A set of materials, for example, may use one comprehensive teacher's edition or a set of guides—one for each theme or topic in a program. Mixed sets of commercial and teacher-made materials may not include a teacher guide at all. Be exact and list only those material items actually available for review. These are the assets for the delivery of instruction— and contribute to what the teacher does in her daily practice.

If different stakeholders (e.g., administrator, supervisor, teacher) are completing the inventory, it is important that all reviewers come together

Figure 4.3 Sample Inventory of a Set of Curriculum Materials

Category	Definition	Primary Items	Check	Amount
Teacher Materials	Resources to guide and aid instruction	Teacher Guide(s)	✓	8; one for each theme
		Big Books	✓	8; one for each theme
		Read-Aloud Books	✓	16; 2 per theme
		Picture/Word Card Sets	✓	8; one for each theme
		Charts	✓	4 poem cards
		Props		
Student Materials	Resources for student use with/without the teacher	Little Books		
		Manipulatives	✓	1 set of letter tiles 1 bingo game 2 sets of flannel board figures
		Practice Materials	✓	1 book of reproducible pages for practice
Curriculum Description	Text that describes the rationale, goals, standards base, and instructional activities of the program/set of materials	Research Summary	✓	
		Goals Description	✓	
		Standards Chart		
		Description of Instructional Activities	✓	
Scope/ Sequence	An organizer that shows which major skills should be taught and the time frame for teaching them	Chart	✓	
Assessment Materials	Resources for ongoing assessment of skills	Assessment Tasks		
		Student Forms		
		Record Forms		
		Interpretation		

Category	Definition	Primary Items	Check	Amount
Home-School Materials	Resources that link the curriculum to the home	Parent Letter	✓	1 per theme
		Home Activities/ Games	✓	1 per theme
		Tips for Parents	✓	
Multimedia Materials	Digital resources to support instruction and student practice	Software		
		e-Books		
		Audio/CDs	✓	1 song per theme
		DVDs		
Professional Development Materials	Descriptive information about the research base, models of instruction, and links to professional organizations	Research Summaries	✓	3: phonological awareness, alphabet knowledge, and print knowledge
		Examples of Instructional Sequences		
		Recommendations for Professional Resources		

after completing an inventory to share what they have found *before* moving onto Part II. All reviewers should confirm that they identified material items in the proper categories so that when completing Part II they rate the same material items, thus avoiding inconsistencies and confusion in scoring.

Finally, indicate if the review is being conducted on a complete or an incomplete set of materials/program. This matters because incomplete sets can lead to incomplete reviews that often yield a limited view of the strengths and weaknesses of a set of curriculum materials. A complete set of materials for review, on the other hand, helps reviewers develop a complete picture of what program has to offer—and in the end provides a fairer "test" of the product.

IDENTIFYING WHAT TYPE OF CURRICULUM MATERIALS

In early childhood literacy, the types of curriculum materials and programs developed for early literacy experiences and instruction vary widely. This is understandable given the patchwork nature of early childhood education, ranging from public/private school programs to Head Start agencies to day care programs to in-home care. The ELMS inventory encourages identifying kinds of materials undergoing a review. The tool identifies four broad types of early literacy curriculum materials: (1) *publisher-based;* (2) *embedded* in a larger, comprehensive curriculum; (3) *prepackaged* early literacy instructional materials; and (4) *a mixed set* of commercial, prepackaged, and teacher-made materials. These major types of curriculum materials are summarized in Figure 4.4. More in-depth descriptions of the use of ELMS to review such types of curriculum materials can be found in Chapter 6.

Figure 4.4 Types of Curriculum Material Sets/Programs

Types	Characteristics
Publisher-Based	All materials used are part of a publisher's salable program
Embedded	Materials are embedded in a comprehensive curriculum
Prepackaged	Materials are organized in sets of packaged material that address specific skills (e.g., alphabet knowledge)
Mixed	Materials from multiple sources constitute the program, including published/commercial, prepackaged sets and teacher made

CHAPTER 4 REVIEW

The initial step in using the ELMS review tool is to complete an inventory of the material items available for language and literacy instruction. The prudent among us take careful inventory of curricular assets and give a faithful accounting to those who depend on these materials for daily practice. Taking inventory involves (a) locating identifying information about the curriculum materials, (b) checking the availability of items and in what amount, (c) determining the completeness of a set of materials, and (d) identifying the kind of set or program undergoing review. It is an essential first step to a substantive review that describes the strengths and weaknesses of curricular materials applied to early literacy instruction. After the inventory of materials you take a closer look at the *quality* of the materials; this is Part II of the tool and is explained in Chapter 5. (See Resource B, Glossary of Terms, for definitions of curriculum material related concepts.)

Part I: To-Do List

☐ Gather all materials
☐ Work through one category at a time
☐ Check the column if items are available
☐ Record the number of items available for review, if applicable
☐ Share findings for consistency if there are multiple reviewers
☐ Check the product type most represented

Examining the Quality of Curriculum Material

5

Arriving at a conclusion about quality takes both time and effort— but, most important, it takes guidance in recognizing what quality looks like!

The first part of ELMS, the *Inventory of Materials,* allows reviewers to identify what a set of materials or program contains and in what amount, and in this respect examines the quantity of curriculum materials. But educators need to be concerned not only with *quantity* but also with the *quality* of materials designed for early literacy instruction. Quality in a product is hard to define, although we often know it when we see it (or use the product).

In Part II of the ELMS tool—*Quality of Materials Rating*—quality is defined according to three criteria applied to the primary items in eight categories of materials: (a) availability of primary items in a category, (b) the capacity or volume of available primary items in a category, and (c) the usability of primary items available in a category. Guidelines for evaluating these criteria are provided in Figure 5.1.

Figure 5.1 Guidelines for Rating Quality of Materials

Criterion	Guidelines
Availability	The product should provide all or most of the primary material contents of a category.
Capacity	The product should demonstrate capacity in the category, i.e. the ability to supply enough primary material items to do the job.
Usability	The primary items of a product should demonstrate practical characteristics in three areas: • *Construction.* Primary items should be well organized, easy to use, readable, and durable. • *Appropriateness.* Primary items should provide information/align with the developmental range of the students, be free of gender and racial/ethnic stereotyping, and support English-language learners. • *Appeal.* Primary items should be attractive for intended audiences; capable of engaging them.

Evidence of quality is rated on a 0–3 point scale for each criterion where a rating of 3 indicates high quality and 0 is low quality. Reviewers use the criteria descriptors along with their own professional judgment to inspect the materials and determine a quality rating. A cautionary note: Reviewers should use evidence as the foundation of their judgments to the extent possible and call on their professional experience to inform their decision making; they should avoid "overthinking" (or second guessing) their rating decisions.

A QUALITY RATING WALK-THROUGH

Determining the quality of curricular materials is not an exact science. In this section we "walk through" the decision-making process that results in a quality rating for a category of materials in a program. The brief walk-through illustrates the blend of art and science when making determinations about quality of primary items in a curriculum product. It also serves as a model to follow when examining other categories of curriculum materials.

The type of curriculum product under review in this walk-through is a publisher-based early literacy program. The focus is on the Teacher Materials category that we inventoried in Chapter 2. It is reproduced below (see Figure 5.2).

Figure 5.2 Inventory of Teacher Materials Category

Category	Type of Item	Check	Amount
Teacher Materials	Guide	✓	8; one for each theme
	Big Books	✓	8; one for each theme
	Read-Aloud Books	✓	16; 2 per theme
	Picture/Word Card Sets	✓	8; one for each theme
	Charts	✓	4 poem cards
	Props		

The reviewer approaches the rating task by asking guiding questions related to each criterion (see Figure 5.3).

1. What primary items are available in the category? To answer this question, the reviewer refers to the inventory and notes that most, but not all, of the primary items are available. She assigns a rating of *2* on this criterion.

2. What is the capacity of primary items available in the category? Here the reviewer is attempting to rate the power of the category to support instruction based on the available items. This criterion grapples with this issue: *Of the primary items available, are there enough to do the instructional job?* From a resource perspective, a high-capacity product (one that is plentiful with respect to the primary items available) offers more instructional support for the teacher than a low-capacity product (one that is lacking with respect to the items available) in this category. The reviewer draws on two sources of information to make a rating. She refers first to the inventory data and observes that several instructional supports for each theme are provided (Guides, Big Books, Read-Aloud Books, Picture/Word Cards), but she also notes that there are fewer charts and no props. She uses her professional knowledge and experience to consider the value-added benefit of ready-made charts and at-hand props in day-to-day instruction. Integrating these data sources, she assigns a rating of *2,* indicating the moderate capacity of this category for instructional support. Of the items available, she reasons, there is a sufficient amount to accomplish effective instructional delivery.

3. What is the usability of primary items available in the category? To rate this criterion, the reviewer must take into account the construction,

appropriateness, and appeal of the material items (see Figure 5.3) She inspects the guides, for example, for organization, ease of use, readability, and durability. She sees that easy-to-read plans for each unit and for each week within a unit are provided, but the text boxes that surround the instructional pages are distracting. The guides are fairly lightweight and include tabs for easy reference—the paper stock, though, seems flimsy, especially for the front/back panels, which can lead to a tattered manual with continued use. The books include topics and text within the developmental range of young children; they also are available in Spanish. Of the eight Big Books, however, only two are informational texts. Book illustrations and artwork are attractive and colorful; the picture/word cards contain vivid, real-life photos, and the accompanying words are written in large-sized, clear block print. Considering these practical characteristics of the material items in this category, she assigns a *2* on this criterion. In general, the usability of materials is very good for routine classroom use.

Figure 5.3   Walk-Through Example

Quality Criteria											
Availability of Items				Capacity Judgment of How Much				Usability of Items			
3	2	1	0	3	2	1	0	3	2	1	0
All	Most	Some	No	High	Moderate	Limited	Low	Superior	Very Good	Good	Poor

CALCULATING THE QUALITY OF MATERIALS RATING SCORE

Once ratings for each category have been determined, the reviewer follows a 4-step procedure and (1) determines the total points for each column, (2) determines the total points for each criterion, (3) sums criterion points, and (4) computes the percentage of criteria met as an indicator of overall quality. See a worked example in Resource C.

INTERPRETING THE QUALITY OF MATERIALS RATING

What does the final percentage actually mean as a rating? The percentage expresses the relative quality of the primary items in a set of curriculum materials or a program as a product. This is to say that it describes to what extent and how much the curriculum product (the set of primary items) has to offer its users, as well as its practicality for use in classroom application. Often overlooked, these are nonetheless important curricular considerations because they influence the instructional delivery system. For example, products with lower percentages would suggest lower quality. Products with higher percentages offer more robust sets of primary materials that can support access to instruction, opportunity to teach and learn, and consistent use in the instructional program. Such products are, in a word, *high performers*. They can add motivation and strength to the implementation of effective language and literacy programs. Resource C has a complete worked example of quality ratings and the percentages.

CHAPTER 5 REVIEW

When examining the qualities of a product, such as a set of curriculum materials, there are two fundamental questions: What does it include, and what is it like? The *Quality of Materials Rating* provides this information, organizing the characteristics of a product around criteria of availability, capacity to deliver, and usability. Systematically rating what a set of curriculum materials has to offer in the eight categories of primary items yields an overall rating of product quality. This rating is an indicator of *potential*, that is, what the set of primary materials affords its users. Next, you will examine the quality of the instructions that accompany the materials.

Part II: To-Do List

- ❏ Review Resource C, which is an example of a completed Part II
- ❏ Organize materials into the eight categories
- ❏ Determine the availability of primary items by referring to Part I
- ❏ Rate the capacity of the available items to support instruction
- ❏ Rate the usability of the items
- ❏ Determine the total points for each column
- ❏ Determine the total points for each criterion
- ❏ Add up the points
- ❏ Compute the percentage of criteria met
- ❏ Record the findings from Part II on the Summary Sheet, Part IV

Analyzing the Guidance Provided in Curriculum Materials

6

Give people enough guidance to make the decisions you want them to make. Don't tell them what to do, but encourage them to do what is best.

Guidance consists of the *written directions* provided to use curriculum materials for instruction. It is the *set of instructions* for the *instruction*. The quality of guidance is important because it can support fidelity of implementation or how well instruction is implemented per the curriculum design (O'Donnell, 2008). Guidance can help teachers use a program as it is "supposed to be used," as intended by the developer. It contributes to the integrity, adherence, or quality of program delivery. For new or inexperienced teachers, the guidance provided can be vital to assisting them in delivery of instruction in ways that the publisher intended.

Part III of the ELMS tool analyzes guidance provided in science-based early literacy skill domains, focusing on 20 instructional items of early literacy best practice in seven categories (see Figure 6.1). These items are derived from early literacy research and represent proven or promising practices at this point in time. The analysis detects the presence of these items indicative of effective practice for each category in the written guidance of a lesson. In other words, the analysis provides the evidence that evidence-based practices are present in the instructional guidance for teachers. This is critical information because sets of curriculum materials and programs have strengths and weaknesses in this regard. There is no one wholly comprehensive set of language and literacy curriculum materials or a perfect program. Educators need to be aware of *gaps in guidance* and find ways to close these gaps in instructional delivery.

Figure 6.1 Description of Early Literacy Categories and Instructional Items

Category	Items	Description
Oral Language	Clear procedures for shared reading before, during, and after reading	Procedures describe what to do before reading (e.g., discuss the book cover); during reading (e.g., ask/answer questions); after reading (e.g., ask to find favorite part)
	Clear procedures for developing listening comprehension skills	Procedures describe how to encourage listening to gain understanding of the intended meaning of the text: connecting to prior knowledge, summarizing, predicting, asking questions, inferencing, and identifying main ideas
	Multilevel questions for teacher-child discussion	Sample questions stimulate discussion at literal, interpretive, and applied levels
	Prompts for language facilitation	Prompts encourage confirming, clarifying, elaborating, and extending child language
Vocabulary	Sets of words for instruction	A range of vocabulary words is available for instruction, including basic concept, root, and disciplinary content words.
	Activities that develop vocabulary consciousness	Activities support awareness that words may have different meanings based on their context and a desire to know more words.
	Clear procedures for vocabulary instruction	Procedures describe how to teach new words (e.g., contextualized method)
	Child-friendly definitions of words	Words are defined simply and connected to childhood experience
Phonological Awareness	Clear procedures for teaching sound awareness in words	Procedures describe explicit steps for teaching sound awareness (e.g., recognizing and producing rhyming words).
	Activities for segmenting sentences and words	Activities support hearing words in sentences, compound words, syllables in words, and beginning sounds in words.

Category	Items	Description
Alphabet Letter Knowledge	Clear procedures for teaching letter names and sounds	Procedures describe explicit steps for teaching how to hear and say name letters; initial letters in words
	Activities for naming letters and sounds	Activities support name writing, letter identification games, forming letters, and exploring alphabet books.
Print Knowledge	Clear procedures for developing concepts of print	Procedures describe how to teach book handling; print components (e.g., letter); directional conventions; print functions (e.g., story comes from print, not pictures).
	Activities for exploring mixed-genre books and texts	Activities support shared reading; book browsing; solo pretend reading
Developmental Writing	Clear procedures for interactive writing	Procedures describe steps for engaging children in joint writing activities, such as *sharing the pen* (helping children spell and write some words) and *side-by-side teaching,* such as supporting ideas, talking about writing, and repeating what children say/write.
	Clear procedures for name writing and simple words	Procedures describe steps for helping children write their names and other simple words, such as *forming* letters, saying letter names, *making* letter sounds, *listening* for letter sounds, and *matching* letter names and sounds.
	Activities for functional and compositional writing	Activities support functional writing (everyday writing for a particular purpose) and compositional writing (forming a whole piece; to bring meaning to an idea).
Differentiated Instruction (i.e., students who are developmentally different, culturally diverse, ELL)	Options for meeting student needs in whole-group instruction	Options describe additions to instruction in whole-group settings, such as repetitions, clarifications, and examples.
	Organization for small-group instruction	Organization or "how to" arrange for small-group instruction is described, such as scheduling and selecting children.
	Activities for small-group instruction	Activities support targeted skill instruction that supplements whole-group instruction.

Most often guidance is found in a teacher manual or program guide. It varies from general outlines of instructional steps to detailed scripts of what to say and do during instruction. It is not necessary, nor is it realistic, to analyze every set of directions for instruction in an entire set of curricular materials or a commercial program. A representative sample of lessons can be used to locate evidence of curriculum guidance that helps teachers provide instruction in science-based early literacy skills. What constitutes a sample of lessons, however, can be confusing since the early childhood literacy curriculum is often arranged into units or themes that may consist of multiple lessons. The Harcourt Trophies Pre-Kindergarten program, or HT-PreK (Harcourt, Inc., 2005/2007), for example, consists of 5 units, 25 themes and 125 daily lessons. Each theme contains 5 lessons—and in this case the *theme* is a suitable unit of analysis. An eclectic early literacy curriculum used in the Sunny Days Preschool comprises approximately 72 lessons, requiring 2 days for each. Here the individual lesson may serve as an appropriate unit of analysis.

To ensure equity across programs yet stay manageable in terms of time, the ELMS tool requires at least 10% of a unit of analysis for review purposes. In the HT-PreK program (Harcourt, 2005/2007), for example, two themes (10 daily lessons) would provide an adequate sample, whereas in the eclectic program above a total of seven lessons would suffice. In a sequential program, where lessons build on one another, select samples from the beginning, middle, and end of the program. In a nonsequential program, select lessons in any order from the total program. Keep in mind that most daily lessons are quite short and can be analyzed relatively quickly for evidence of quality features in the skill domains.

Reviewers must use professional knowledge and judgment to complete this part of the tool. Oftentimes, inferences must be made. For example, in one set of materials reviewed the specific words, "small group" and "large group" were not used in the teacher manual. As reviewers looked for evidence of differentiation, including directives for providing small- and large-group instruction, they had to use their professional knowledge and infer that these activities were designed for meeting the needs of different children in both small- and large- group settings.

CONDUCTING AN ANALYSIS

Once a sample set of lessons has been identified, an analysis of guidance can be conducted on the sample. The analysis involves a two-step procedure of (1) locating evidence in the lesson sample and (2) marking the analysis sheet to indicate presence of guidance on the instructional item. The lesson excerpt in Figure 6.2 illustrates how evidence is located in a lesson sample (Harcourt, 2005, p. 8).

Figure 6.2 Example of Locating Evidence in a Lesson Sample

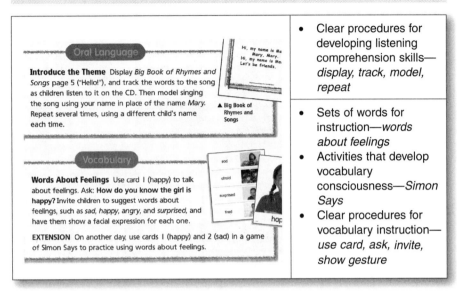

This evidence is then marked as present in the sample (Sample 1) on the Analysis Sheet as indicated in Figure 6.3. The process of locating and marking the presence of evidence in all the samples is then completed.

COMPUTING THE CATEGORY SCORE

The goal of the guidance analysis is to determine the relative presence of instructional items indicative of evidence-based practices by category in the sample. Said another way, you want to determine how strong the guidance is in a specific category of early literacy skill instruction. The more instructional items present in the product, the stronger the guidance to support the implementation of instruction.

To compute the relative presence of guidance by category:

- Score the frequency of each item across the sample set (analysis forms accommodate up to three samples on each sheet);
- Determine the average number of items present in the sample set *(Divide the total number of features by the sample size. Total Score ÷ Sample Size; Note: Round the average number of items present to a whole number.)*;
- Calculate the percentage of quality features in each category. *Divide the average of features present by the total number of features possible. Average ÷ Total Possible. For example: 3 (average) ÷ 4 (total number of features possible) = 75%.*

Figure 6.3   Identifying Evidence of Components

Category/Item	Sample Check if Present in the Sample			Score
Sample	1	2	3	
Oral Language *guidance provides*				
• Clear procedures for shared reading before, during, *and* after reading				
• Clear procedures for developing listening comprehension skills	✓			
• Questions for teacher-child discussion	✓			
• Prompts for language facilitation	✓			
Total Score				
Average Score				
Percentage				
• Sets of words for instruction	✓			
• Activities that develop vocabulary consciousness	✓			
• Clear procedures for vocabulary instruction	✓			
• Child-friendly definitions of content words				
Total Score				
Average Score				
Percentage				

The computation of the relative presence of items in the Oral Language category for an analysis of three samples is shown in Figure 6.4. (See a complete worked example in Resource D.)

Based on these samples, the guidance in this set of curriculum materials addresses a majority of evidence-based instructional items in oral language foundations for the learn-to-read process, but it lacks clear procedures for shared reading across all its phases (before, during, after).

Figure 6.4 Computing the Percentage of Items Present

Category/Item	Sample Check if Present in the Sample			Score
Sample	1	2	3	
Oral Language *guidance provides*				
• Clear procedures for shared reading before, during, *and* after reading				0
• Clear procedures for developing listening comprehension skills	✓	✓	✓	3
• Questions for teacher-child discussion	✓		✓	2
• Prompts for language facilitation	✓	✓	✓	3
Total Score				8
Average Score				8 ÷ 3 = 2.66
Percentage				3 ÷ 4 = 75%

Those implementing the curriculum need to consider this gap in the guidance and find ways to address it with other guidance sources, such as professional texts and journals. This example is an illustration of how important both the percentage score and the notes taken are to making appropriate curricular decisions. While the score identifies a *gap in guidance*, more detailed notes can shed light on what procedures are provided even if they are not present at all phases of the lesson. Taking notes while completing the tool and subsequently taking the time to discuss them with other reviewers (to the extent possible) is an important part of the curriculum material review process.

INTERPRETING AN ANALYSIS OF GUIDANCE

The analysis shows the strengths and weaknesses of the guidance, that is, the set of instructions for program delivery, as determined against a set of criteria—the evidence-based items of instructional practice in essential early literacy skill categories. It maps, in short, the topography of a set of curriculum materials—its peaks and valleys, so to speak. This is critical information not only for planning instruction but also for identifying professional development activities that improve the use of a curriculum resource. Categories with lower percentages of items, for example, will require augmentations to ensure full coverage of the skill domain—and teachers will need professional development to learn how to incorporate these resources effectively into daily instruction. In this respect, the analysis works toward the larger goal of language-rich and rigorous curricula in early childhood settings, and it serves as a mechanism for improving professional knowledge and effective practices.

CHAPTER 6 REVIEW

Analyzing the guidance is a critical look at the written instructions for the teacher to use in the delivery of instruction. The reviewer locates and identifies items indicative of evidence-based practice in early literacy skill domains. The process involves (a) studying the teacher manual and analyzing the directions for instruction for each category, (b) determining what items are evident and marking the guidance sheet, and (c) computing a category score. This straightforward analysis can be done rather efficiently and provides sufficient evidence to determine strengths and weaknesses of the written directions that support program delivery. What *is* and *is not* present in the guidance also informs professional development in the effective use of curriculum materials. In Chapter 7 you will summarize the results of Parts I–III of ELMS and interpret the scores comprehensively.

Part III: To-Do List

- ❏ Review Resource D, which is an example of a complete Part III
- ❏ Review Figure 6.1 *Descriptions of a Category*
- ❏ Identify sample set of lessons
- ❏ Work through one category at a time
- ❏ Place a checkmark next to the item there is evidence present
- ❏ Score the frequency of each item across the sample set
- ❏ Determine the average number of items present in the sample set (Divide the total number of features by the sample size)
- ❏ Calculate the percentage of quality features in each category (Divide the average of features present by the total number of features possible)
- ❏ Record percentages for each domain at the end of Part III
- ❏ Transfer percentages for Analysis of Guidance and Average Percentage to Part IV

Arriving at the Final Rating

7

The score is so much more than a number.

The results of the quality survey of materials and the analysis of program guidance are averaged to yield a *product review* of the curriculum/program as a set of materials for early literacy instruction. In general, the product review describes how well a set of materials *performs* when assessed against a set of criteria that describes features of quantity and quality of materials, and guidance. Like all consumers, educators seek high-performing materials that work well in their particular settings.

COMPLETING A PRODUCT REVIEW

Completing Part IV, *Quality Performance Rating*, is relatively straightforward. Percentages earned on the Quality Rating of Materials and the Program Guidance Analysis, respectively, are summed and averaged to compute a final score. As shown in figure 7.1, the final score indicates a product rating on a scale from "low" to "good" to "very good" or "exceptional" in terms of performance, which is defined by the overall quality of materials and the extent to which guidance (set of directions) for program delivery is evidence based.

Figure 7.1   Product Review Performance Chart

Exceptional	Very Good	Good	Low
≤ 100%	≤ 75%	≤ 50%	≤ 25%

For example, a review of the XYZ Program indicated a final percentage score of 75% (Materials Survey = 70%; Guidance Analysis = 80%) thus the program review indicates a very good level of performance. We can interpret this to mean that the XYZ Program makes available a variety of primary items in major categories of materials in sufficient numbers to show very good usability features (e.g., organization); the guidance is trustworthy, reflecting what we know about effective early literacy instruction. Basic descriptors for each level of performance that aid interpretation of the final score are summarized in Figure 7.2.

Figure 7.2   Descriptors to Guide Interpretation of a Final Score

Level of Performance	Descriptors	
	Quality of Materials	*Program Guidance*
Exceptional	High availability of primary items in most categories	High percentage of evidence-based components in all skill domains
	High volume of materials in most categories	
	Superior usability for many primary items in most categories	
Very Good	Very good availability of primary items in most categories	High percentage of evidence-based components in most of the skill domains
	Sufficient volume of materials in most categories	
	Very good usability of many primary items in most categories	
Good	Good availability of primary items in some categories	Adequate percentage of evidence-based components in most of the skill domains
	Limited volume of materials in some categories	
	Good usability of some primary items in some categories	
Low	Some availability of primary items in some categories	Low percentage of evidence-based components in most of the skill domains
	Low volume of materials in most categories	
	Poor usability of many primary items in most categories	

OBSERVING PATTERNS OF INSTRUCTION

Interpretations of a product review can go one step further. The percentages calculated for skill domains in the program guidance analysis can yield *patterns of instruction* in a set of materials. Three general patterns tend to emerge: (1) a code-related pattern that emphasizes phonological awareness, alphabet letter knowledge, print knowledge, and writing (particularly name writing); (2) a meaning-related pattern that foregrounds oral language, vocabulary, and writing, specifically writing composition activities; and (3) an integrated pattern that shows a fairly even distribution of code-related and meaning-related components across skill domains. Evidence of these basic patterns of instruction is useful because it shows how different programs offer different "menus" of early literacy instruction. This kind of information is valuable in making decisions about the relative strength of a set of curriculum materials/program for meeting the specific needs of a specific group of children in a specific educational setting. A few examples of code-related and meaning-related patterns follow.

Letters and Sounds Code-Related Pattern

Curriculum materials characterized by this pattern show a larger proportion of instructional content directed to phonological awareness and alphabet letter knowledge than other skill categories, such as print knowledge, vocabulary, and/or language comprehension. The emphasis in these programs is on learning to hear sounds in language and words, and to identify alphabet letter names and sounds.

Sounds, Letters, and Concepts of Print Code-Related Pattern

Programs that exhibit this pattern show a relatively even mix of phonological awareness skills and alphabet letter knowledge, along with basic concepts of print, such as directional conventions, print components (e.g., concepts of letter and word), and punctuation conventions. Proportionally less instruction is directed to vocabulary and/or language comprehension skill areas.

Language Comprehension Meaning-Related Pattern

Sets of curriculum materials that show characteristics of this pattern focus the largest proportion of instruction on oral language comprehension skills, such as using social interaction rules, grammatical rules, turn-taking, sharing ideas, responding to talk, and so on, over other skill categories, such as phonological awareness. The emphasis is on using language effectively to satisfy social and communicative needs, as well as meeting the demands of school-like routines, such as shared book reading.

Vocabulary and Language Comprehension
Meaning-Related Pattern

Curricular programs with this pattern show proportionally more instruction on vocabulary and language comprehension areas than other skill categories, such as phonological awareness or alphabet letter knowledge. The program may offer a vocabulary collection and target specific vocabulary words for instruction.

CHAPTER 7 REVIEW

The foundations of literacy are laid in early education that prepares children for the phonologic, alphabetic, semantic, and syntactic demands of learning to read, along with an eagerness to undergo the task. Early literacy curricular materials and products can contribute to children's early literacy development by offering strong content and by providing multiple opportunities for engagement with books and print. The ELMS tool supports this goal by providing assessment information for a product review and for observing patterns of instruction in a curriculum resource. The informational value is twofold: (1) A product review indicates a general level of performance in terms of quantity and quality of materials and guidance strengths, and (2) patterns of instruction provide program developers and educators with information for making informed decisions about program selection and implementation. In these ways, the tool helps professionals to select and apply program materials flexibly in early literacy instruction. In the final chapter we describe the process and studies involved in the development of ELMS.

Part IV: To-Do List

☐ Make sure all summary scores are transferred to Part IV
☐ Determine an overall level of performance
☐ Establish the overall pattern of instruction

Technical Information

8

Although the journey was long and the effort never ending, the result is a well-designed tool that has the potential to create positive educational change.

everal desk studies and small-scale field studies were conducted to develop the technical adequacy and usability of the ELMS tool over several years. In an initial pilot desk study (Roskos, Vukelich, & Neuman, 2005), the original prototype of the tool (referred to as ELPRT) was applied to a nine-program sample drawn from a pool of 15 programs identified by the United States Department of Education as commercially available early literacy programs.[1] Using a systematic procedure, the curriculum and early literacy content quality features of the sample were assessed by trained graduate assistants. Inter-rater reliability of tool application ranged between 70 and 80%. Results showed that the tool identified key curricular elements in the program sample, as well as the distribution of quality features of early literacy content in the program guidance, although there was some overlap between coding categories. Drawbacks were noted in the tool's usability, such as the considerable time commitment in locating and recording evidence of quality instructional features in teacher materials.

---

1. In 2002, the Office of Elementary and Secondary Education at the United States Department of Education prepared a list of 15 programs as preliminary information for a study of early childhood early literacy programs.

Based on the initial pilot desk study, the tool was modified and further tested on a three-program sample by the principal researchers (Roskos & Vukelich, 2007). Procedures for data entry were clarified and streamlined into a Microsoft Excel software application that allowed easy entry of page numbers to document evidence of quality instructional features and to convert raw frequency data into graphic displays. Additionally, categories were color-coded to visually highlight patterns in the instructional materials. The interactive software improved the accuracy and efficiency of data entry, and it supported the interpretation of the results. Sets of directions for data entry, analysis, and interpretation were expanded to include more explicit coding guidance and sample profiles to aid interpretation.

Two follow-up field studies were conducted using this computer-based version of the tool. In a comprehensive early childhood service site, a program director and nine teachers examined program samples for purposes of evaluating several early literacy programs under consideration for adoption. Following a one-day training on the tool, three-member teacher teams spent two weeks conferring and completing reviews of assigned programs. Reconvening the teams, the program director guided a discussion of the results and worked with the team to rank-order the early literacy programs for adoption. User feedback supported the reliability of the tool in identifying quality features, but also highlighted practicality issues related to the software application. A side benefit of the tool was also reported. In the course of the training on the tool, review teams engaged in lots of discussion about what constituted evidence, how to tag statements of evidence, definition of terms (e.g., target vocabulary), clarity and organization of the instructional guidance, and issues of developmental appropriateness related to early literacy instruction. Application of the tool, in short, led to professional learning opportunities.

At a university-based preschool site, the program director and staff had recently adopted a new early childhood curriculum with embedded early literacy instruction. The program director used the tool to gather additional information about the early literacy instructional materials included. She oriented her teaching staff to the tool. Together the group selected a 25% sample from the beginning, middle, and end of the early childhood curriculum. Using a portion of their regular staff meeting time, they searched for evidence of quality features related to literacy content, entering the data into the Microsoft Excel spreadsheet. The meeting time, although brief, allowed them opportunity to discuss the strengths and gaps they found across categories and to consider ways to enhance the instructional materials as needed. In this respect, the director reported, use of the tool facilitated a kind of "on the spot" professional development and planning that informed their overall curriculum implementation.

As in previous field trials, the reliability of the tool with training proved adequate (70% range), but the computer-based version was reported as hard to manipulate for purposes of data entry and to "read" for purposes of interpretation. Users also reported a preference for some analyses over others. Evaluating quality features of curricular elements and instructional sequences, for example, were less preferable than identifying quality features of guidance in the teacher materials.

The authors (Roskos, Lenhart, and Noll) conducted a third round of modifications to the tool in fall 2008, primarily to improve overall reliability and usability in preschool settings. The tool was reorganized into a four-part design that (1) inventoried types of instructional materials for review, (2) surveyed quality of instructional materials, (3) analyzed essential content features of program guidance, and (4) combined survey and analysis scores to determine an overall quality rating. To formatively test the integrity of the revised tool, the researchers reviewed a popular commercial program. Based on this review, further adjustments were made to the tool. For example, a notes column was added to the materials survey, a glossary was developed to clarify the description of specific materials, and instructional items were added to the early literacy skill domains, particularly in writing. In addition, the rating scales were revised to better describe salient features of quality materials. The tool was then field-tested by several early childhood educators, including two higher-education faculty, three teachers in a local university-based preschool, a public preschool teacher, and a Head Start director. Each applied the review tool to instructional materials they had used previously, had available to them, or were currently using in their program. Instructional materials varied in dates of publication, publishers, and range of instructional materials; some were commercial and others included purchased and teacher-created curriculum materials. Over a two-week period, the reviewers applied the tool, using a checklist to comment on its technical adequacy and usability. Feedback was generally positive. Reviewers found the tool to be useful in looking at the quality features of instructional materials. Adjustments were made to the tool to develop the inventory, clarify terminology in the materials survey, improve scoring procedures, add directions, and improve documentation of observations on the record forms.

A revised form of the tool (now referred to as ELMS) was launched in fall 2010 and tested on a commercial program sample. The revised tool consisted of four parts to rate quantity and quality of curricular materials: (1) an inventory that identified the amount of material items in eight categories, (2) a quality of materials survey that rated material categories on a 5-point scale, (3) an analysis of guidance that located evidence of 20 instructional items, and (4) a performance rating scale that combined the scores of the materials survey and guidance analysis. A five-member team, consisting of three preschool teachers and two kindergarten teachers, applied each section of the tool to the sample, individually determining ratings and negotiating differences among themselves. Inter-rater reliability (within 1 score point) was 71% for the Quality of Materials Survey and 90% on the guidance analysis. This "test" session, monitored by the two of the authors, yielded copious observations on the content, organization, clarity, workability, and utility of the tool, and led to another major revision that streamlined portions of the tool and improved the scoring system. In brief, the quality of materials portion of the tool was revised to (a) better align it with the inventory information; (b) organize it around three well-defined criteria of material quality—availability, volume (defined as capacity of materials to do the instructional job), and usability; and (c) rate the criteria on a 0–3 scale, with 0 indicative of low quality and 3 of high quality. Overall, the scores for the materials survey and the guidance analysis were converted from raw scores to percentages, which provided a stronger foundation for a combined score average in determining the overall performance of a curriculum product. The revised tool was subjected to a round of author-led simulations with extant data from prior trials to "test" the workability of the changes. Results showed a more organized, accurate, useful, manageable, and promising tool for reviewing curriculum materials. At this point, we consider the alpha phase of tool development complete.

Resource A

ELMS Tool

A Tool for Early Literacy Program Materials Review

Product Name(s):	Copyright
Reviewer(s):	
Date:	

Part I. Inventory of Materials

Category	Definition	Primary Items	Check if present	Amount
Teacher Materials	Resources to guide and aid instruction	Teacher Guide(s)		
		Big Books		
		Read-Aloud Books		
		Picture/Word Card Sets		
		Charts		
		Props (e.g., puppet)		
Student Materials	Resources for student use with/without the teacher	Little Books		
		Manipulatives (e.g., letter tiles)		n/a
		Practice Materials		
Curriculum Description	Text that describes the rationale, goals, standards base, instructional activities of the program/set of materials	Research Summary		n/a
		Goals Description		n/a
		Standards Reference Chart		n/a
		Description of Major Instructional Activities		n/a

Category	Definition	Primary Items	Check if present	Amount
Scope/ Sequence	An organizer that shows which major skills should be taught and the time frame for teaching them	Chart		n/a
Assessment Materials	Resources for ongoing assessment of skills	Assessment Tasks With Directions		
		Student Forms		
		Record Forms		
		Interpretation of Results		n/a
Home-School Materials	Resources that link the curriculum to the home	Parent letters		
		Home Activities & Games		
		Tips for Parents		n/a
Multimedia	Digital resources to support instruction and student practice	Software		
		e-Books		
		Audiotapes/CDs		
		DVDs		
Professional Development Materials	Descriptive information about the research base, models of instruction, and links to professional organizations	Research Summaries		

(Continued)

(Continued)

Category	Definition	Primary Items	Check if present	Amount
		Examples of Instructional Sequences		n/a
		Recommendation for Professional Resources		n/a

Check the product type most representative of the set of materials or program.

☐ Commercial language and literacy program

☐ Embedded early literacy program in a comprehensive curriculum

☐ Prepackaged assortment of early literacy materials

☐ Mixed assortment of prepackaged and teacher-made early literacy materials

Complete Set of Materials: ☐ Yes   ☐ No

Part II. Quality of Materials Rating

Category	Primary Items	Quality Criteria											
		Availability of items				Capacity judgment of how much [1]				Usability of items [2]			
		3	2	1	0	3	2	1	0	3	2	1	0
		All	Most	Some	No	High	Moderate	Limited	Low	Superior	Very Good	Good	Poor
Teacher Materials	• Guide(s) • Big Books • Read-Aloud Books • Picture, Word Card Sets • Charts • Props												
Student Materials	• Little Books • Manipulatives • Practice Materials												
Curriculum Descriptions	• Research Summary • Goals Description • Standards Chart • Description of Instructional Activities												
Scope/ Sequence	• Chart												

(Continued)

61

(Continued)

Category	Primary Items	Quality Criteria											
		Availability of items				Capacity judgment of how much [1]				Usability of items [2]			
		3	2	1	0	3	2	1	0	3	2	1	0
		All	Most	Some	No	High	Moderate	Limited	Low	Superior	Very Good	Good	Poor
Assessment Materials	• Assessment Tasks • Student Forms • Record Forms • Interpretation of Results												
Home-School Materials	• Parent Letters • Home Activities & Games • Tips for Parents												
Multimedia	• Software • E-Books • Audio/CDs • DVDs												

Category	Primary Items	Quality Criteria											
		Availability of items				Capacity judgment of how much [1]				Usability of items [2]			
		3	2	1	0	3	2	1	0	3	2	1	0
		All	Most	Some	No	High	Moderate	Limited	Low	Superior	Very Good	Good	Poor
Professional Development Materials	• Research Summaries • Examples of Instructional Sequences • Recommendations for Professional Resources												
Column Total													
Criterion Total													
Sum of Criterion Scores:													
Total Percent (Sum of Criterion Scores ÷ 72):													

Steps:

1. To judge availability, determine if all items listed in the category are available (100%); most items are available (≥ 50%); some are available (≤ 50%); none are available (0%).

2. To judge capacity, determine the volume of *the available items* (those that a program package actually contains) as high (enough to do the job well); moderate (enough to do the job adequately); limited (barely enough to do the job) or low (not enough to do the job).

3. To judge usability, consider the qualities of the material items available in the program package and assign a rating. *Refer to the Inventory of Materials as needed.*

[1] Use data from Inventory to inform this judgment; High = Enough to do job well; Moderate: enough to do job adequately; Limited: Barely enough; Low = Not enough

[2] Based on features of (i) construction (organization, ease of use, readability, durability); (ii) appropriateness (within developmental range of students; free of gender and racial/ethnic stereotyping; adaptable for ELL); (iii) appeal (attractive to audience; capable of engaging intended audience)

Part III. Analysis of Guidance

Each item is worth 1 point.

Category/Item	Sample Check if present in the sample			Score
Sample	1	2	3	
Oral Language *guidance provides*				
• Clear procedures for shared reading before, during, *and* after reading				
• Clear procedures for developing listening comprehension skills				
• Questions for teacher-child discussion				
• Prompts for language facilitation				
Total Score				
Percentage				
Vocabulary *guidance provides*				
• Sets of words for instruction				
• Activities that develop vocabulary consciousness				
• Clear procedures for vocabulary instruction				
• Child-friendly definitions of content words				
Total Score				
Percentage				
Phonological Awareness *guidance provides*				
• Clear procedures for teaching sound awareness in words				
• Activities for segmenting sentences and words				
Total Score				
Percentage				
Alphabet Letter Knowledge *guidance provides*				
• Clear procedures for teaching letter names and sounds				
• Activities for naming letters and their sounds				
Total Score				
Percentage				

Print Knowledge *guidance provides*				
• Clear procedures for developing concepts of print				
• Activities for exploring print in mixed genre books and texts				
Total Score				
Percentage				
Writing *guidance provides*				
• Clear procedures for interactive writing				
• Clear procedures for name writing and simple words				
• Activities for functional writing				
Total Score				
Percentage				
Differentiated Instruction *guidance provides*				
• Options to meet student needs in whole group instruction				
• Organization for small group instruction				
• Activities for small group instruction				
Total Score				
Percentage				
Average Percentage				

Domain	%	Domain	%	Domain	%
Oral Language		Alphabet Letter Knowledge		Differentiated Instruction	
Vocabulary		Print Knowledge			
Phonological Awareness		Writing		Average	

Part IV. Quality Performance Rating

Part II: Quality of Materials Rating: __%

Part III: Analysis of Guidance: __%

Average Percentage   __%

Performance (use the chart below):

☐ Exceptional   ☐ Very Good   ☐ Good   ☐ Low

Exceptional ≤ 100%	Very Good ≤ 75%	Good ≤ 50%	Low ≤ 25%

INTERPRETATION OF PERFORMANCE RATING

Level of Performance	Descriptors	
	Quality of Materials	Program Guidance
Exceptional	High availability of primary items in most categories	High percentage of evidence-based components in all skill domains
	High volume of materials in most categories	
	Superior usability for many primary items in most categories	
Very Good	Very good availability of primary items in most categories	High percentage of evidence-based components in most of the skill domains
	Sufficient volume of materials in most categories	
	Very good usability of many primary items in most categories	

Level of Performance	Descriptors	
	Quality of Materials	*Program Guidance*
Good	Good availability of primary items in some categories	Adequate percentage of evidence-based components in most of the skill domains
	Limited volume of materials in some categories	
	Good usability of some primary items in some categories	
Low	Some availability of primary items in some categories	Low percentage of evidence-based components in most of the skill domains
	Low volume of materials in most categories	
	Poor usability of many primary items in most categories	

Resource B

Glossary of Terms

Alphabet knowledge. The ability to name, write, and identify the sound of alphabet letters.

Big books. An oversized book designed for reading in a group setting, where children can see the written words that represent speech.

Commercial program. An inclusive collection of student books, teacher manuals, and supplemental materials produced by a publishing company for use in the classroom.

Desk study. Generally an investigation of the available facts and figures relevant to a specific issue; often described as Phase 1 of a site investigation that forms the basis of preliminary risk assessment. Specific to tool design, it provides early recognition of characteristics in sufficient detail to inform further design and field application.

Developmental writing. The development of marks children use for the purpose of conveying a message in print.

Developmentally appropriate. An approach to education that promotes children's active exploration of the environment. The focus is on the child as a developing human being and lifelong learner who constructs meaning and knowledge through interaction with others, friends and family, materials, and setting.

Evidence-based. An empirical, data-based approach to early literacy instruction focused on core language and literacy skills that are the predictors of primary grade reading achievement.

Explicit instruction. A systematic instructional approach that has a set procedure derived from research. It is teaching that is structured, intentional, and focused on specific learning outcomes.

Language comprehension. The ability to listen and speak with understanding.

Manipulatives. Small objects that can be handled and used by young children, such as puppets, puzzles, miniature figures, and letter tiles.

Mini-books. Reproducible, theme-related small books that children can take home and keep.

Mixed-genre. Different kinds of texts, including narrative, poetry, nonfiction, song, and plays.

Multimedia. A combination of several types of resources, such as books, picture cards, charts, CDs, software, and so on, included in a commercial program to make it engaging and comprehensive; also the presentation of visual and audio information in different formats.

Multisensory objects. Objects that engage children through more than one of the senses, such as sandpaper letters.

Narrative. A story expressed orally or written that is fictional; usually includes two or more events that build to some sort of climax, and then goes on to reach a resolution.

Phonological awareness. Sensitivity to sounds in words and the ability to manipulate them; conscious awareness of the sound structure of speech as opposed to its meaning.

Print knowledge. Conceptual knowledge of the purposes and conventions of print: concept of word; print awareness; and knowledge of reading terms, rules, and procedures.

Realia. Real objects or artifacts used to relate classroom teaching to real life, such as photographs, a tool, or other authentic items.

Shared reading. A reading activity in which a teacher reads text such as a big book while a group of learners look at the text being read and follow along; children may chime in as the text is read.

Socio-dramatic play. An advanced form of play in literacy-enriched play centers where children take on roles and act out make-believe stories and situations; reflects the following features: imaginary situation, explicit roles, symbolic use of objects, implicit rules, and language sustained for at least 10 minutes

Tier 1 intervention. Curriculum, activities, and routines that are part of teacher instructional and managerial practices that positively influence the rate of learning and child engagement.

Tier 2 intervention. Supplemental, small-group instruction to improve outcomes for children who are not responding satisfactorily to Tier 1 instruction.

Vocabulary. Words an individual knows and can use; words used in speaking (expressive vocabulary) and/or recognized in listening (receptive vocabulary).

Resource C

Example of Completed Part II

Quality of Curriculum Materials

Steps

1. To judge availability, determine if all items listed in the category are available (100%); most items are available ($\geq$ 50%); some are available ($\leq$ 50%); none are available (0%).

2. To judge capacity, determine the volume *of the available items* (those that a program package actually contains) as high (enough to do the job well), moderate (enough to do the job adequately), limited (barely enough to do the job), or low (not enough to do the job).

3. To judge usability, consider the qualities of the material items available in the program package and assign a rating.

Refer to the Materials Inventory as needed.

		Quality Criteria											
		Availability of Items				Capacity Judgment of How Much[a]				Usability of Items[b]			
		3	2	1	0	3	2	1	0	3	2	1	0
Category	Primary Items	All	Most	Some	No	High	Moderate	Limited	Low	Superior	Very Good	Good	Poor
Teacher Materials	• Guide(s) ✓ • Big Books ✓ • Read-Aloud Books • Picture, Word Card Sets • Charts ✓ • Props		✓					✓			✓		
Student Materials	• Little Books • Manipulatives • Practice Materials ✓			✓			✓				✓		
Curriculum Descriptions	• Research Summary • Goals Description ✓ • Standards Chart ✓ • Description of Instructional Activities ✓		✓				✓					✓	
Scope/Sequence	• Chart	✓					✓				✓		
Assessment Materials	• Assessment Tasks • Student Forms • Record Forms • Interpretation of Results				✓				✓				✓

Quality Criteria

Category	Primary Items	Availability of Items — 3 All	2 Most	1 Some	0 No	Capacity Judgment of How Much[a] — 3 High	2 Moderate	1 Limited	0 Low	Usability of Items[b] — 3 Superior	2 Very Good	1 Good	0 Poor
Home-School Materials	• Parent Letters ✓ • Home Activities & Games • Tips for Parents			✓				✓				✓	
Multimedia	• Software • E-Books • Audio/CDs • DVDs				✓				✓				✓
Professional Development Materials	• Research Summaries • Examples of Instructional Sequences • Recommendations for Professional Resources				✓				✓				✓
Column Total		3	4	2	0	8	6	2	0	0	6	2	0
Criterion Total		**9**				**8**				**8**			

Sum of Criterion Scores: 25

Total Percent (Sum of Criterion Scores ÷ 72): 35%

Notes:

a. Use data from Inventory to inform this judgment;
   High = Enough to do job well
   Moderate = Enough to do job adequately
   Limited = Barely enough
   Low = Not enough

b. Based on features of (a) construction (organization, ease of use, readability, durability), (b) appropriateness (within developmental range of students, free of gender and racial/ethnic stereotyping, adaptable for ELL), and (c) appeal (attractive to audience, capable of engaging intended audience)

Resource D

Example of Completed Part III

Analysis of Guidance

Directions

Each item is worth 1 point.

Category/Item	Sample Check if present in the sample			Score
Sample	1	2	3	
Oral Language *guidance provides*				
• Clear procedures for shared reading before, during *and* after reading	x			1
• Clear procedures for developing listening comprehension skills	x	x	x	3
• Questions for teacher-child discussion	x		x	2
• Prompts for language facilitation	x	x	x	3
Total Score				9
Average Score				3
Percentage				75%

(Continued)

(Continued)

Category/Item	Sample Check if present in the sample			Score
Sample	1	2	3	
Vocabulary *guidance provides*				
• Sets of words for instruction	x	x	x	3
• Activities that develop vocabulary consciousness	x	x	x	3
• Clear procedures for vocabulary instruction	x	x	x	3
• Child-friendly definitions of content words	x			1
Total Score				10
Average Score				3
Percentage				75%
Phonological Awareness *guidance provides*				
• Clear procedures for teaching sound awareness in words	x			1
• Activities for segmenting sentences and words		x	x	2
Total Score				3
Average Score				1
Percentage				50%
Alphabet Letter Knowledge *guidance provides*				
• Clear procedures for teaching letter names *and* sounds		x		1
• Activities for naming letters and their sounds	x		x	2
Total Score				3
Average Score				1
Percentage				50%
Print Knowledge *guidance provides*				
• Clear procedures for developing concepts of print	x	x	x	3
• Activities for exploring print in mixed genre books and texts				
Total Score				3
Average Score				1
Percentage				50%

Category/Item	Sample Check if present in the sample			Score
Sample	1	2	3	
Writing *guidance provides*				
• Clear procedures for interactive writing		x	x	2
• Clear procedures for name writing and simple words				
• Activities for functional writing				
Total Score				2
Average Score				1
Percentage				33%
Differentiated Instruction *guidance provides*				
• Options to meet student needs in whole group instruction	x	x	x	3
• Organization for small group instruction				
• Activities for small group instruction	x	x	x	3
Total Score				6
Average Score				2
Percentage				67%
Average Percentage				57%

Domain	%	Domain	%	Domain	%
Oral Language	75%	Alphabet Letter Knowledge	50%	Differentiated Instruction	67%
Vocabulary	75%	Print Knowledge	50%		
Phonological Awareness	50%	Writing	33%	**Average**	57%

Resource E

Organizers for Planning and Facilitating Reviews

FORMAL TEAM APPROACH CHECKLIST

As a team prepares to evaluate curricula using ELMS, complete the steps below. During the review, check off each task to ensure completion of every step of the process:

- ☐ Determine the team leader.
- ☐ Determine contributing members of the team; then record and share contact information with the entire group.
- ☐ Gather data about local policies and needs.
- ☐ Recognize and record the most critical goals and priorities of the organization.
- ☐ Create a timeline for completion of the tasks.
- ☐ Complete all four parts of the ELMS tool.
- ☐ Reconvene the group to discuss your findings and in order to revisit goals and priorities.
- ☐ Determine future action steps (i.e., make plans for purchasing a program that was evaluated, redesigning use of current programs, planning and designing future professional development, etc.)

SMALL-GROUP APPROACH CHECKLIST

As your small group prepares to evaluate curricula using ELMS, complete the steps below. During the review, check off each task to ensure completion of every step of the process:

- ☐ Determine contributing members of the team; then record and share contact information with the entire group.
- ☐ Gather data about local policies and needs.
- ☐ Recognize and record the most critical goals and priorities of the organization.
- ☐ Create a timeline for completion of the tasks.
- ☐ Complete all four parts of the ELMS tool.
- ☐ Reconvene the group to discuss your findings and in order to revisit goals and priorities.
- ☐ Determine future action steps (i.e., make plans for purchasing a program that was evaluated, redesigning use of current programs, planning and designing future professional development, etc.).

ON YOUR OWN CHECKLIST

As you prepare to evaluate curricula using ELMS, complete the steps below. During the review, check off each task to ensure completion of every step of the process:

- ☐ Gather data about local policies and needs.
- ☐ Recognize and record the most critical goals and priorities.
- ☐ Create a timeline for completion of the tasks.
- ☐ Complete all four parts of the ELMS tool.
- ☐ Reflect on your findings, and revisit goals and priorities.
- ☐ Determine future action steps (i.e., make plans for purchasing a program that was evaluated, redesigning use of current programs, planning and designing future professional development, etc.).

TEAM REVIEW: RECORDING GENERAL INFORMATION

Evaluation Team Members

**Lead Member: _____ Position: _____

Contact Information: _____

_____

Team or Small-Group Members

1. Team Member: _____ Position: _____

Contact Information: _____

_____

2. Team Member: _____ Position: _____

Contact Information: _____

_____

3. Team Member:_____ Position: _____

Contact Information: _____

_____

4. Team Member: _____ Position: _____

Contact Information: _____

_____

5. Team Member: _____ Position: _____

Contact Information: _____

_____

TEAM REVIEW: POLICY AND NEEDS ORGANIZER

Part I: State/Local Policy Information

**Part II: High/Low Priorities to
Consider Before, During, and After the Team Review**

High Priorities

As a team, small group, or individual, list all of the high priorities that the team believes should drive this evaluation process (e.g., for your team, it may be a high priority that the instructional materials you select represent a culturally mixed group of people within their student materials, among other needs).

Low Priorities

Include any qualities and/or components that are not necessarily of high priority to your team or group. Take into account what materials or programs you already have in place.

TEAM REVIEW: TIMELINE FOR COMPLETION PLANNER

Date of meeting: _____

In the table below, record the action steps, the person responsible for the action steps, and the deadline for completion of each task.

Action Steps	Person(s) Responsible	Deadline

Resource F

Case Study Example of a Team Review

Although the sites, reviewers, materials, and uses of the ELMS tool can be numerous and varied, this chapter illustrates just one specific example of the ELMS tool in action.

In this chapter, the authors describe a full-day review using the most recent version of the tool.

THE APPROACH

On a weekday in October, seven literacy professionals were brought together at a local university to review the 2007 version of Harcourt Trophies Pre-Kindergarten program, using the ELMS tool. The small-group approach, described in Chapter 6, was used, and members included several early childhood literacy coaches, an early childhood parent liaison, a pair of elementary teachers with a range of teaching experiences from preK to Grade 1, and an educational consultant who was also a former teacher. Two of the authors of this tool served as facilitators for the review.

THE TYPE OF MATERIALS REVIEWED

In order to prepare for the task, the facilitators gathered all of the Harcourt program materials, a publisher-based early literacy program. The materials were currently being used in a local Head Start preschool program, the same location at which many of the members of the review team were employed. Of the seven participants, several were already familiar with the program as it was currently being used as a major part of their core reading program.

FAMILIARIZING PARTICIPANTS WITH ELMS

Because the participants were all knowledgeable in the field of early childhood literacy, little time was devoted to exploring the general chapters or sections describing early literacy research that helped to shape the tool. Rather, at the start of the review, participants were given a brief overview of the ELMS tool. The facilitators briefly reviewed each section of the tool, including the organization, format, and utility of each section. Participants were also provided with time to read specified portions of the pertinent chapters that accompany the tool. The atmosphere was organized yet informal, and participants were encouraged to stop and ask questions or make comments at any time during the review.

USING PART I: INVENTORY OF CURRICULUM MATERIALS

For the first section of the tool, the *Inventory of Curriculum Materials*, participants worked cooperatively to inventory the contents of the Harcourt Trophies program. Conversation and comments were encouraged, as each participant filled out his or her own copy of the ELMS tool. Much conversation was centered on whether to categorize some program materials as teaching or student materials. During this stage of inventorying the materials, it was not critical that each participant place the items in the same category; however, when participants would later complete Part II, comparison of scores would have been very difficult if some participants had categorized materials in different ways. So consensus needed to be reached during this part of the review process to ensure that completion of Part II would proceed smoothly.

A book that included all of the reproducibles for the program was one such item that some reviewers considered teaching materials and others considered student materials. The argument was given that the teacher actually makes the copies of the reproducibles, so these participants felt that the book should be categorized under teaching materials. On the other hand, others felt that since the students would be the ones actually using, or completing the worksheets, the book should be categorized as student materials. After a short time discussing the issue, a general consensus was reached that everyone would include these materials in the

Student Materials section of the tool, due to the fact that the students would actually be *using* the materials. It was determined that it was critical that all participants categorize components in the same sections so that scoring could easily be compared across categories, and less important in which category something was placed.

During this inventory, it was also discovered that there were materials within the program that the publisher had designated for dual purposes. When participants came across lap books provided by the publisher, the participants' conversations started to question the purpose or use of the books. It was decided that the group would need to explore the teacher manuals in order to find the publisher's intended purpose for these pieces of literature. After several minutes of flipping through the teacher manuals, participants came across pages in the book where the publisher had stated that the lap books were to be used by the teacher first and then placed in the classroom library for student use. So indeed this specific material could be categorized as both teaching and student materials on the tool. Once again, for the purpose of this review, it was determined that it was more important that everyone sort these lap books in the same category and less important *which* category was chosen. All reviewers agreed to categorize these books as teaching materials.

It was advantageous to complete this first section of the tool together as a group and to know what procedures and portions of the tool lay ahead. If the participants had not explored the tool in its entirety at the beginning of the review day, they would not have realized the importance of making sure that everyone categorized each publisher-provided material in the same category so that when the *quality* of each material was evaluated in the second section of the tool, participants were actually rating the quality of the same pieces of the product. Otherwise, it would have been very difficult to compare scores across areas and across reviewers.

During this stage of the review process, it was also discovered that certain pieces of the program were missing. The literacy coaches who participated in the review stated that they knew there were pieces that came with the program, but they were not currently being provided to classroom teachers for use in their classrooms. On the notes section of the inventory, the participants recorded the fact that a few materials were listed for use within program materials, but they were not currently being used in classrooms. It was determined that there was no need to investigate these pieces further if they were not going to be provided to the early childhood teachers who were currently using this program.

USING PART II: QUALITY OF CURRICULUM MATERIALS

After familiarizing themselves with materials provided by the publishers of this program, the participants were given instructions about how to proceed to the next step of the process. For this stage of the review, the facilitators directed the participants to work more independently as they looked closely at each of the materials found within each category on the ELMS tool in order to rate their quality. The participants could rate the product materials on a scale of 0–5, with a score of 0 being the lowest range quality and 5 being the highest quality. Reviewers were encouraged to take detailed notes about each category while completing the tool. These notes contributed to rich conversation and critical analysis later when the group discussed their findings.

Participants spent considerable time reviewing the teaching materials that accompanied the Harcourt curriculum, including the teacher guide and teaching resources, as this was viewed as one of the most important pieces of the core program. After recognizing how much time was being spent on the teacher guides, the facilitators intervened by reminding the participants that the third and final section of the tool was designed to look closely at the directives and guidance provided to teachers in the teacher guide. Participants were encouraged to rate the quality of the teacher materials overall, and then to move onto other categories, such as the student materials, curriculum descriptions, scope and sequence, and assessment materials.

Once all participants had completed Part II, the small group discussed this section of the tool. For some categories, there was much agreement about the overall quality of some of the Harcourt materials. For example, after discussion including both numerical scores and descriptive support for scores given, the small group arrived at the conclusion that the teacher materials and curriculum descriptions were of relatively high quality. The group also determined that the lowest scoring areas of program materials included the scope and sequence charts, multimedia, and professional development materials.

In other categories, more discussion was needed to arrive at a more conclusive overall score. For example, there seemed to be much disagreement among reviewers as to the overall quality of the assessment materials. Half of the group rated the assessment materials as high quality, while the other half felt that these materials were of mid-range quality. A discussion followed that allowed the reviewers to provide their support for their ratings. This healthy discussion allowed participants to enter into a deep and powerful discussion of what educators should want from a meaningful and effective assessment program. It was also a time for those educators who were more experienced and well read in the area of assessments to share what they knew about the research-based supporting assessment practices. This is an illustration of how powerful the *process* of using the ELMS tool can be when stakeholders and experts come together as a group to converse about the materials being considered or used.

In another area of disagreement among ratings, the reviewers' teaching philosophies created a variance in scores. The reviewers scored the student materials category across the entire rubric range. During discussion of this variance, it was discovered that the main material that reviewers placed in this category was the reproducible book that had masters of worksheets to be completed by students during lessons throughout the year. During the discussion, it was discovered that various members of the review group had strong feelings for and against the use of worksheets. Some reviewers felt that worksheets are simply "busy work" used by ineffective teachers to keep students busy while the teacher met with groups or individuals, and that worksheets held little educational value. Therefore, these reviewers had rated the materials as low quality. Other reviewers disagreed and had looked beyond the fact that they were worksheets. These reviewers viewed worksheets as a means for teachers to provide students with an opportunity to independently perform a task that had been taught by the teacher previously. These educators felt that independent practice was essential to the gradual release of responsibility model used within classrooms. It was determined by the group that it was necessary to go back to the teacher manual to see how these reproducible worksheets were integrated into the overall lessons. The group decided that the format of a worksheet was not as important as the evidence that the activities and materials were of high quality. Were the worksheets high quality in that they matched the lesson objectives, were developmentally appropriate, were clear and easy for students to use, and fit into the gradual release of responsibility model for instruction? The team worked together to find this evidence in the teacher manuals, and then they were able to reach a conclusion about the quality of the student materials. Although this took more time and effort beyond the time originally given to complete the tool, it was well worth it. All members came away from the activity with a deeper understanding of how worksheets can enhance learning if evaluated in the right ways.

USING PART III: ANALYZING THE GUIDANCE
PROVIDED IN CURRICULUM MATERIALS

In order to prepare for the last section of the tool, the facilitators had pre-selected three sets of lessons to be evaluated by all participants. In order to shorten the process, skill categories were assigned to only two or three individual participants, rather than assigning each participant the task of evaluating each of the seven research areas.

This part of the review process takes time, patience, and attentiveness to complete. Users of the tool must look closely at the guidance provided by the publisher, and also must read the descriptions provided in the accompanying user guide carefully to see if there is evidence that evidence-based practices are present. Each participant went to work looking at the selected lessons from the teacher manuals while recording how many of the evidence-based practices were included in each of the three lessons.

Participants had been familiarized with how to tally the total scores and percentages before they started, and had reviewed the examples provided in the user guide. However, if participants needed assistance, the facilitators provided support when necessary, including providing calculators to help tally the scores of each section. During this process, participants were almost completely silent, working diligently to record the presence of guidance for teachers. The silence was broken a few times for questions that arose. For example, when one participant arrived at the Vocabulary portion of the tool, she wondered if the term "set of words" meant the same as "list of words." The group determined that a set of words would be the same as a list. This short, targeted discussion helped to ensure that all reviewers were on the same page as they completed the review. The setting helped to encourage this—and should be considered by any group considering a review. In this instance, all reviewers were in the same location for the review process, which allowed for conversations throughout completion of each part of the tool.

Although variances in scores are inevitable, the opportunity to discuss and clarify these inconsistencies was valuable to critically evaluating the strengths and weaknesses of the program materials.

Participants were encouraged to take notes about what they found, or failed to find, within the teacher manuals. Many participants recorded the evidence they found to support each category. Once all participants had completed their use of the tool, these notes became a springboard for discussion among the whole group. Most often the discussions led back to research. Often these individuals made comments about what they did not like about the program and how they might change the directives given by the program to better align with research. It became clear during this ELMS review process that the *actual process itself* had led to very meaningful and rich discussions that would benefit any group of professionals determined to amp up the instruction taking place within classrooms that were using these commercial products. This supports the use of ELMS with staff members who actually use, or may use the programs being reviewed, as well as the use of ELMS as a springboard for professional development.

CONCLUSION OF THE REVIEW PROCESS

At the end of the review day, participants tallied their final scores for the program on the *Quality Performance Rating.* Reviewers shared around the table any final or conclusive questions, comments, and concerns about the program itself, including the quantity and quality of the product materials and the guidance provided within the teacher manuals. Summative discussions centered around the strengths and weaknesses of the program itself. The discussion then led to action steps that could be taken to ensure that the weakest areas of the program could be enhanced within the classroom setting. Moving beyond the scores assigned to the program and into plans for the future was an important and natural next step in the process of evaluating materials that were currently being used at the preschool site. Action steps were discussed, some which involved changing teaching behaviors or adding teaching materials to supplement weak areas within the program currently being used. All reviewers left with a better understanding of what should be expected of a high-quality, evidence-based literacy curriculum and how this particular set of materials met these demands.

References

Adams, J. M., Foorman, R. B., Lundberg, I., & Beeler, T. (1998). *Phonemic awareness in young children.* Baltimore, MD: Paul H. Brookes.

Barnett, D. A., VanDerHeyden, A. M., & Witt, J. C. (2007). Achieving science-based practice through response to intervention: What it might look like in preschools. *Journal of Educational and Psychological Consultation, 17,* 31–54.

Biemiller, A. (2003, Spring). Oral comprehension sets the ceiling on reading comprehension. *The American Educator, 27,* 23.

Biemiller, A., & Boote, C. (2005). An effective method for building meaning vocabulary in primary grades. *Journal of Educational Psychology, 98*(1), 44–62.

Bodrova, E., & Leong, D. J. (2007). *Tools of the mind.* Upper Saddle River, NJ: Pearson.

Bohn, C. M., Roehrig, A. D., & Pressley, M. (2004). The first days of school in the classrooms of two more effective and four less effective primary-grades teachers. *The Elementary School Journal, 104,* 269–287.

Both-deVries, A. C., & Bus, A. G. (2008). Name writing: A first step to phonetic writing? Does the name have a special role in understanding the symbolic function of writing? *Literacy Teaching and Learning, 12,* 37–55.

Bowman, B. T., Donovan, M. S., & Burns, M. S. (Eds.). (2001). *Eager to learn: Educating our preschoolers.* Washington, DC: National Research Council.

Burns, S., Griffith, P., & Snow, C. (1999). *Starting out right: A guide to promoting children's reading success.* Washington, DC: National Academy Press.

Clay, M. (1975). *What did I write?* Portsmouth, NH: Heinemann.

Corcoran, T., & Goertz, M. (1995). Instructional capacity and high performance schools. *Educational Researcher, 24,* 27.

Diamond, A., Barnett, W. S., Thomas, J., & Munro, S. (2007). Preschool program improves cognitive control. *Science, 318*(5855), 1387–1388.

Dickinson, D., & Neuman, S. B. (2006). *Handbook of early literacy research, VII.* New York: Guilford.

Dodge, D., Colker, L., Heroman, C., & Bickart, T. (2002). *The creative curriculum for preschool.* Washington, DC: Teaching Strategies.

Ellis, E. S., & Worthington, L. A. (1994). *Research synthesis on effective teaching principles and the design of quality tools for educators* (Technical Report No. 5). Eugene: University of Oregon, National Center to Improve the Tools of Educators. Retrieved from ERIC database. (ED386853)

Ferreiro, E., & Teberosky, A., (1982). *Literacy before schooling.* Portsmouth, NH: Heinemann Educational Books.

Fisher, C. W., Berliner, D. C., Filby, N. N., Marliave, R., Ghen, L. S., & Dishaw, M. M. (1980). Teaching behaviors, academic learning time, and student achievement. In C. Denham & A. Lieberman (Eds.), *Time to learn.* Washington, DC: National Institute of Education.

Foorman, B. R., & Torgeson, J. (2001). Critical elements of classroom and small group instruction promote reading success in all children. *Learning Disabilities Research and Practice, 16*(4), 203–212.

Frede, E. C. (1998). Preschool program quality in programs for children in poverty. In W. S. Barnett & S. S. Boocock (Eds.), *Early care and education for children in poverty: Promises, programs and long-term outcomes* (pp. 77–98). Buffalo, NY: SUNY Press.

Gentry, J. R. (2005). Instructional techniques for emerging writers and special needs students at kindergarten and Grade 1 levels. *Reading and Writing Quarterly, 21,* 113–134.

Glover, M. (2009). *Engaging young writers—Preschool–Grade 1.* Portsmouth, NH: Heinemann.

Hall, T., Strangman, N., & Meyer, A. (2011). *Differentiated instruction and implications for UDL implementation.* Retrieved from http://aim.cast.org/learn/historyarchive/backgroundpapers/differentiated_instruction_udl

Harcourt, Inc. (2005/2007). *Trophies Pre-Kindergarten.* Orlando, FL: Author.

Hart, B., & Risley, T. (1995). *Meaningful differences in the everyday experience of young American children.* Baltimore: Paul H. Brookes.

Hart, B., & Risley, T. (2003). The early catastrophe: The 30 million word gap. *American Educator, 27,* 4–9.

Hirsch, Jr., E. D. (2006). *The knowledge deficit: Closing the shocking education gap for American children.* New York: Houghton Mifflin.

International Reading Association (IRA). (1998). Learning to read and write: Developmentally appropriate practices for young children. A joint position statement of the International Reading Association (IRA) and the National Association for the Education of Young Children (NAEYC). *The Reading Teacher, 52*(2), 193–216.

Justice, L., & Vukelich, C. (Eds.). (2008). *Achieving excellence in preschool literacy instruction.* New York: Guilford.

Levin, I., & Bus, A. G. (2003). How is emergent writing based on drawing? Analyses of children's products and their sorting by children and mothers. *Developmental Psychology, 39,* 891–905.

Lonigan, C. J., Burgess, S. R., & Anthony, J. L. (2000). Development of emergent literacy and early reading skills in preschool children: Evidence from latent variable longitudinal study. *Developmental Psychology, 36,* 596–613.

Marulis, L. M., & Neuman, S. B. (2010). The effects of vocabulary intervention of young children's word learning: A meta-analysis. *Review of Education Research, 80*(3), 300–355.

McBride-Chang, C. (1999). The ABCs of the ABCs: The development of letter-name and letter-sound knowledge. *Merrill-Palmer Quarterly, 45,* 285–308.

McCardle, P., Scarborough, H., & Catts, H. (2001). Predicting, explaining and preventing children's reading difficulties. *Learning Disabilities Research & Practice, 16*(4), 230–239.

McGee, L. M. (2004). *The role of wisdom in evidence-based preschool literacy curriculum.* Keynote Address at the National Research Conference, San Antonio, TX.

McGee, L. M. (2007). *Transforming literacy practices in preschools.* New York: Scholastic.

Memmel, M., Ras, E., Jantke, J. K., & Yacci, M. (2007). Approaches to learning object oriented instructional design. In A. Koohang & K. Harman (Eds.), *Learning objects and instructional design* (pp. 281–325). Santa Rosa, CA: Informing Science Press.

Mol, S. E., & Bus, A. G. (2011, March). To read or not to read: A meta-analysis of print exposure from infancy to early adulthood. *Psychological Bulletin, 137*(2), 267–296.

Morrow, L. M. (2005). *Literacy development in the early years* (5th ed.). New York: Pearson.

NAEYC & NAECS/SDE. (2004). *Early childhood curriculum, child assessment and program evaluation: Building an accountable and effective system for children birth through age eight.* Retrieved from http://www.naeyc.org/positionstatements/cape

National Early Literacy Panel (NELP). (2009). *Early beginnings: Early literacy knowledge and instruction.* Jessup, MD: National Institute for Literacy.

National Reading Panel. (2000). *Teaching children to read: An evidence-based assessment of the scientific research literature on reading and its implications for reading instruction.* Retrieved from http://www.nichd.nih.gov/publications/nrp/report.cfm

Neuman, S. B., Roskos, K., Wright, T., & Lenhart, L. (2007). *Nurturing knowledge: Building a foundation for school success by linking early literacy to math, science, art, and social studies.* New York: Scholastic.

O'Donnell, C. L. (2008). Defining, conceptualizing, and measuring fidelity of implementation and its relationship to outcomes in K–12 intervention research. *Review of Educational Research, 78*(1), 33–84.

Opening the world to literacy (OWL). (2005). Upper Saddle River, NJ: Pearson.

Perfetti, C. A. (1987). Language, speech and print: Some asymmetries in the acquisition of literacy. In R. Horowitz & S. J. Samuels (Eds.), *Comprehending oral and written language* (pp. 355–370). New York: Academic Press.

Pianta, R. C., Cox, M. J., & Snow, K. L. (Eds.). (2007). *School readiness & the transition to kindergarten in the era of accountability.* Baltimore, MD: Paul H. Brookes.

Roskos, K. A., & Christie, J. F. (2007). *Play and literacy in early childhood: Research from multiple perspectives.* New York: Lawrence Erlbaum.

Roskos, K. A., Tabors, P. O., & Lenhart, L. A. (2009). Joining oral language and early literacy. In K. A. Roskos, P. O. Tabors, & L. A. Lenhart (Eds.), *Oral language and early literacy in preschool: Talking, reading, and writing* (pp. 1–6). Newark, DE: International Reading Association.

Roskos, K., & Vukelich, C. (2007). Quality counts: Design and use of an early literacy program review tool. In L. Justice & C. Vukelich (Eds.), *Achieving excellence in preschool literacy instruction.* New York: Guilford.

Roskos, K., Vukelich, C., & Neuman, S. B. (2005, June). *Are early literacy programs research-based? A critical review of the evidence.* NAEYC Research Conference, Miami, FL.

Rowe, D. W. (2008). Development of writing abilities in childhood. In C. Bazerman (Ed.), *Handbook of research on writing* (pp. 401–419). New York: Lawrence Erlbaum.

Schickedanz, J. A. (1999). *Much more than the ABCs: The early stages of reading and writing.* Washington, DC: NAEYC.

Shonkoff, J. P., & Phillips, D. A. (2000). *From neurons to neighborhoods: The science of early childhood development.* Washington DC: National Academy Press.

Silverman, R. 2007. A comparison of three methods of vocabulary instruction during read-alouds in kindergarten. *The Elementary School Journal, 108*(2), 97–113.

Snow, C. E., Burns, M. S., & Griffin, P. (Eds.). (1998). *Preventing reading difficulties in young children.* Washington, DC: National Academy Press.

Strickland, D. (1989). A model for change: Framework for an emergent literacy curriculum. In D. S. Strickland & L. M. Morrow (Eds.), *Emerging literacy: Young children learn to read and write* (pp. 135–146). Newark, DE: International Reading Association.

Teale, W., & Sulzby, E. (1986). *Emergent literacy: Writing and reading.* Norwood, NJ: Ablex.

Tomlinson, C. A. (2001). *How to differentiate instruction in mixed-ability classrooms* (2nd ed.). Alexandria, VA: ASCD.

Torgeson, J. K. (2002). The prevention of reading difficulties. *Journal of School Psychology, 40,* 7–26.

Treiman, R. (2000). The foundations of literacy. *Current Directions in Psychological Science, 9,* 89–92.

Vukelich, C., & Christie, J. (2009). How children learn to read and write. In C. Vukelich & J. Christie (Eds.), *Building a foundation for preschool literacy: Effective instruction for children's reading and writing development* (pp. 1–15). Newark, DE: International Reading Association.

Vygotsky, L. S. (1978). *Mind and society: The development of higher mental processes.* Cambridge, MA: Harvard University Press.

Wiggins. G. P., & McTighe, J. (2007). *Understanding by design* (2nd ed.). New York: Prentice Hall.

Wolf, M., Bally, H., & Morris, R. (1986). Automaticity, retrieval processes and reading: A longitudinal study in average and impaired readers. *Child Development, 57,* 988–1000.

Index

CORWIN
A SAGE Company

The Corwin logo—a raven striding across an open book—represents the union of courage and learning. Corwin is committed to improving education for all learners by publishing books and other professional development resources for those serving the field of PreK–12 education. By providing practical, hands-on materials, Corwin continues to carry out the promise of its motto: **"Helping Educators Do Their Work Better."**